Treasures
for the Table

Treasures for the Table

SILVER FROM THE CHRYSLER MUSEUM

Essays by David Revere McFadden
Entries by Mark A. Clark

HUDSON HILLS PRESS • NEW YORK

In Association with The American Federation of Arts

First Edition

© 1989 by the American Federation of Arts
and the Chrysler Museum.

Published in the United States by Hudson Hills
Press, Inc., Suite 1308, 230 Fifth Avenue,
New York, NY 10001-7704.

Distributed in the United States, its territo-
ries and possessions, Canada, Mexico, and
Central and South America by Rizzoli Inter-
national Publications, Inc.
Distributed in the United Kingdom, Eire, Eu-
rope, Israel, and the Middle East by Phaidon
Press Limited.
Distributed in Australia by Bookwise Inter-
national.
Distributed in Japan by Yohan (Western Pub-
lications Distribution Agency).
Distributed in South Korea by Nippon Shuppan
Hanbai.

Editor and Publisher: Paul Anbinder

Copy Editor: Constance Herndon

Indexer: Gisela S. Knight

Designer: David Skolkin/Binns & Lubin

Composition: U.S. Lithograph, typographers

Manufactured in Japan by Toppan Printing
Company

All photographs were taken by Scott Wolff and
Karen Twiddy except:
Statens Konstmuseer (figure 4)
Scott Hyde (figures 1–3, 5, 7, 8)
John Parnell (figure 6)

Library of Congress Cataloguing-in-Publication
Data

Chrysler Museum.
Treasures for the table: silver from the Chrysler
Museum/essays by David Revere McFadden;
entries by Mark A. Clark.—1st ed.
p. cm.
"In association with the American Federation
of Arts."
Bibliography: p.
Includes index.
1. Silverware—Exhibitions. 2. Chrysler
Museum—Exhibitions. I. McFadden, David
Revere. II. Clark, Mark A. III. Title.
NK7107.N67C484 1989
739.2'383074015—dc 19   88-32350
                                                      CIP

ISBN: 1-55595-011-6 (alk. paper)

Contents

List of Colorplates

Foreword

Many years ago I had a professor of Greek art who held up a fifth-century pot and said, "From this pot you can understand all of Greek art." At the time I thought that was a silly statement. In later reflection, however, I began to realize there was some truth in it. The proportions, both in the shape of the pot and in the figures depicted upon it, mirror those in sculpture and painting. Moreover, the rhythms between parts do indeed reflect those sought in architecture. Having seen these relationships, I have looked differently not only upon Greek pots but upon all decorative arts. Often wonderful objects in and of themselves, they can also show us, in microcosm, the world in which they are created.

For example, in savoring the superb George III epergne in the exhibition, one sees the delicate rhythms of rococo plasterwork. The joy in the intricate balancings of solids and voids is like that in the furniture of the period, and the careful composition that leads the eye around the entire piece is similar to that in a freestanding sculpture. Yes, the epergne *is* eighteenth-century England.

Each of these objects of silver was created to be used at the table—tea table or dinner table. They became integral to the daily ceremonies of life. They truly join practicality with beauty, thus heightening existence through their elegant shapes and glittering surfaces.

It is with great pleasure that the Chrysler Museum, in collaboration with the American Federation of Arts, sends these pieces to six other museums. We hope all those who see them will delight in their singular beauties as well as reflect on the worlds they so artfully mirror.

DAVID W. STEADMAN
Director
The Chrysler Museum

Preface

As this catalogue amply illustrates, the Chrysler Museum possesses a rich and comprehensive collection of silver from around the world. Its holdings are particularly strong, however, in the work of British and American silversmiths, including several particularly notable pieces made by the city of Norfolk's own silversmiths. The Museum's delight in presenting these works arises not from local pride, of course, but from the fact of their great rarity—while Norfolk silversmiths were responsible for some of the most beautiful pieces produced in the United States, the destruction wrought on the city by both the Revolutionary and Civil wars meant that very little Norfolk silver has survived into the twentieth century.

A note about the catalogue entries: no attempt has been made here to explain the variety of complicated marking systems for the silver of each country represented. This information is readily accessible in the reference works listed in the bibliography. Individual marks are listed in each entry, however, with a brief explanation of their meanings.

This exhibition and catalogue were made possible by many individuals to whom I would like to extend my gratitude. Harold B. Nelson, Chief Administrator for Exhibitions of the American Federation of Arts, provided invaluable support; without him the exhibition and catalogue would not have been possible. Michaelyn Mitchell, Publications Coordinator of the American Federation of Arts, was also extremely helpful. Special thanks are due to David Revere McFadden, Curator of Decorative Arts at the Cooper-Hewitt Museum, for his informative introduction and his assistance in selecting the objects in the exhibition, and to Constance Herndon for the excellent job she did of editing the catalogue and essays.

I am particularly grateful to Dr. David W. Steadman, Director of the Chrysler Museum, and to Roger D. Clisby, Deputy Director and Chief Curator, whose support for the exhibition was so instrumental in its success. Also among the staff of the Chrysler Museum my thanks go to Chief Librarian Amy Ciccone and her assistants, and to Registrar Catherine Jordan and her assistant, Irene Roughton. I am particularly grateful to Karen Twiddy and Scott Wolff, who photographed the silver —one of the most difficult of materials to capture on film—and would like to recognize Museum Conservator Foy Casper for his special assistance in this task. My admiration and thanks also go to Georgia Lasko,

Curatorial Administrative Assistant, for her preparation of the catalogue information for the editor.

Charles Carpenter, Jr.'s books on Gorham and Tiffany silver were invaluable references during the development of this project, but Mr. Carpenter willingly and generously supplied further information as well. Edward Money, Design Chief for Gorham, Division of Textron, Inc., went out of his way to assist us, as did Patricia G. Bennet of the Charleston Library Association. Finally, I would like to thank Walter P. Chrysler, Jr., whose keen eye and acquisitions informed the collection on which this exhibition is largely based.

MARK A. CLARK
Curator of Decorative Arts
The Chrysler Museum

Acknowledgments

It is with great pleasure that the American Federation of Arts joins with the Chrysler Museum in organizing this exhibition and publishing its attendant publication. The Chrysler Museum's silver collection is rich and comprehensive and can be appreciated as much for its aesthetic merits as for the chronicle it provides of the complex history of silver. It will now be shared with communities across the nation.

Throughout the development of this project, we have worked closely with Mark A. Clark, Curator of Decorative Arts at the Museum, and Roger D. Clisby, Deputy Director and Chief Curator. We are especially appreciative of Director David W. Steadman's support of the project. We are also very indebted to David Revere McFadden, Curator of Decorative Arts at the Cooper-Hewitt Museum, for his assistance in the selection of the objects and his contribution to this catalogue.

AFA staff members Harold B. Nelson, Chief Administrator for Exhibitions, Michaelyn Mitchell, Publications Coordinator, and Sandra Gilbert, Public Information and Promotion Director, have all assisted in the project's organization.

The National Endowment for the Arts, through its support of the exhibition and catalogue, has made the project possible. The catalogue has been additionally supported by the J. M. Kaplan Fund and the DeWitt Wallace Fund through the AFA's Revolving Fund for Publications.

Finally, I wish to thank the museums that will be presenting the exhibition following its opening at the Chrysler Museum: the R. W. Norton Art Gallery, the Columbia Museum, the Columbus Museum, the Munson-Williams-Proctor Institute Museum of Art, the Huntington Galleries, the Albany Museum of Art, and the Society of the Four Arts.

MYRNA SMOOT
Director
The American Federation of Arts

Treasures for the Table: Silver and Dining

*The atmosphere was stifling despite the Venetian blinds and
the porticos; the heat of the apartments was unbearable. It had
proved impossible to serve dinner in the chateau. The dining
room had been moved outdoors and set out amid orange trees,
in a pretty oblong pavilion in white marble, where the air was
cooled by little nearby fountains giving off jets of pure, bright
water. The middle of the table . . . was covered with a dessert
of admirable elegance. A limpid day lingered on in the thousand
rays of a setting sun: the silver table service shone all the
more brightly.*[1]

The ambiance of an elegantly arranged table in the early nineteenth century is vividly evoked in this description of an
evening meal served in the gardens of the Rothschild château
in Boulogne. Garden and dinner settings combine to create a landscape of
visual delight that finds its focus in a table well furnished with shining
silver and porcelains.

Since ancient times the singular delights of the table have served
metaphorically to characterize a wide range of physical and spiritual ex-
perience. And the basic sensual and social pleasures of eating have always
been shaped, in turn, by the larger body of cultural traditions—fashions
and styles, manners and customs, good taste and forms of etiquette. Over
the course of Western history and still today, the habits and protocols
surrounding food and dining—from simple daily ceremonies to highly
elaborate rituals—may express a community's most fundamental economic, political, and religious values. Objects and customs connected
with the preparation, service, and consumption of food provide anthro-
pologists, sociologists, and historians with a rich field of investigation.
We know a great deal today about social history from the evidence of food
and cuisine, and much of this history is recorded in the objects that have
furnished our tables. The tablewares that survive are important documents
for refining our understanding of the evolution of our design and decorative-
arts traditions.

1. Lady Morgan (née Sydney Owenson), a nineteenth-century Irish woman of letters, quoted in Jean-François
Revel, *Culture and Cuisine* (New York: Doubleday, 1982), p. 227.

For over five thousand years silver has enjoyed a privileged place in European society. Over the millennia, it has forged a great many cultural links between sacred and secular activities, enriching the splendor of the domestic and ceremonial occasions with which it has become associated. Not surprisingly, some of the earliest objects made of silver were used in connection with eating and drinking; in fact, the majority of silver objects that survive from ancient times were so used. Some pieces, such as Greco-Roman libation bowls and medieval Communion chalices, were used in religious contexts, while others were important as refinements for the table, making everyday dining into a special event.

Silver's rarity, even when raw and unformed, long ago secured its status as a precious and economically valuable metal. But silver is a material of great practical value to the metalworker and artisan as well—highly malleable, strong when properly alloyed, lustrous, and resistant to corrosion and decay. These same properties, which make silver an ideal medium to work with, easily assumed symbolic resonance, and silver early came to signify such virtues as purity, permanence, and incorruptibility. When fashioned by a skilled artisan into a useful creation—a cup, a chalice, a candlestick—the material and aesthetic qualities of the metal are combined evocatively with the practical and symbolic functions of the object.

In the continuous evolution of its forms and designs, silver has figured prominently in the long socializing and civilizing process of dining. Despite the advent of fast foods, microwave ovens, and disposable plastics, our dining habits are still influenced by the etiquette, dining codes, and vessels developed centuries ago. Many of the tablewares in common use today are direct descendants of those used in ancient times, and we still project social and economic status by the silver we own and display. To a remarkable extent, we remain in close cultural contact with our ancestors by way of this exceptional material.

The Chrysler Museum collection of silver comprises a variety of forms that testify to the historical interplay of practical and symbolic functions. Designs range from the plainest of drinking vessels to grand and imposing objects for display and theatrical table centerpieces of ornate craftsmanship. Some pieces, such as a kiddush cup, were made for ceremonial contexts; others, such as imposing two-handled cups, were used primarily for display rather than actual drinking. But most of the pieces in this collection—beakers and goblets, sauceboats and tureens, baskets, bowls, jugs, and teapots—appeared on their owners' tables, at least until the context of their use shifted from tabletop to museum vitrine.

The Chrysler Museum collection documents the complex history of table silver over the last three centuries, but it is especially rich in eighteenth- and nineteenth-century examples of the silversmith's art. During these two centuries, improving metalworking technologies joined with changing socioeconomic forces to produce an immense quantity of silver designed specifically for the table and dining room. Many of the forms that first gained widespread popularity during the eighteenth century—tureens, tea services, and centerpieces—still serve as paradigms of design for today's silver manufacturers. We can appreciate the objects gathered in this collection, embodying as they do the stylistic idiosyncrasies of the milieus in which they appeared, as fascinating and revealing documents in the history of design.

Several related themes in the development of domestic silver emerged quite early in the history of the metal's use for dining and drinking. One theme readily apparent in the Roman silver disinterred at archaeological sites is the development of specialized forms intended for use with specific foods. Also at this early date a trend arose to assemble sets, or services, of silver that could be used individually as needed or in concert for a larger gathering of diners. A full service of silver was as impressive to the ancient Romans as it was to the wealthy bourgeois businessmen of the nineteenth century. A *ministerium,* or service, proudly owned by an ancient Roman would contain a wide variety of vessels for drinking and eating, ranging from bowls and trays to goblets, ladles, and ewers. Such a service might well include pieces with very different types of ornamental design. The significance of the *ministerium* was its completeness as a functional set, not its stylistic coherence. Seventeenth- and eighteenth-century Europeans, who assembled their own table services from several different craftsmen or workshops, shared this approach to collecting table silver; not until the past century were extraordinary efforts made, and no expense spared, to assure that every piece in a table service matched exactly in pattern and design. These two ideas—specialization and multiplication of elements in a service—have continued to influence silver design down to our own day, and they assumed fundamental importance in the eighteenth and nineteenth centuries when silver became available to a much wider audience.

A third theme that has changed little over the millennia is silver's important function in display. In the ancient world silver was a visible index of personal, familial, and dynastic wealth, and efforts were made to display silver objects in a suitably impressive manner. Although we know less about the ornamental use of silver in the Greco-Roman world than we might wish, telling documents from seventeenth- and eighteenth-century Europe indicate the increasing importance of silver for display purposes. An important precedent for seventeenth-century display, which often reached theatrical levels, was the tiered court cupboard of the fifteenth and sixteenth centuries. On such pieces of furniture—the predecessors of our sideboards—were proudly arranged decorative earthenware, Chinese porcelains, Venetian glass, and silver, either gilded or plain. By the seventeenth century such displays were an essential architectural element for aristocratic households of any pretension and means. Beyond their power to impress, such displays revealed the owner's self-conscious assembly of important objects; these were arranged, sometimes by specialists hired by the household, in strictly ordered sequences. Contempo-

FIGURE 1
Design for a double cup, Nuremberg, Germany, 1581. Bernard Zan. Courtesy of the Cooper-Hewitt Museum, Smithsonian Institution/ Art Resource, New York; Purchase in Memory of Mrs. John Innes Kane, 1945-17-3A.

FIGURE 2
Design for a seventeenth-century silver sideboard, Bologna, Italy. Domenico Bolognese. Courtesy of the Cooper-Hewitt Museum, Smithsonian Institution/Art Resource, New York; Friends of the Museum Fund, 1938-88-2596.

rary prints illustrating such grand displays of silver reveal the importance of a symmetrical arrangement—twice the amount of silver was, of course, needed—to create the most effective and memorable display of personal wealth. In the eighteenth century certain distinguished individuals chose to have their silver included in their painted portraits. Today a prized tea service or tureen is often displayed prominently on a sideboard or buffet, even though it may never be called into active service at table.

Libation bowls used for sacred ceremonies in the ancient world survive in considerable numbers, indicating the perceived affinity between the symbolic metals and the sacred liquids. We can still appreciate this affinity today in kiddush cups and Communion chalices, which are often made of precious metals. Vessels to be used for wine—the "gift of the gods"—were frequently made of silver or gold. For wealthy Greeks and Romans, everyday drinking vessels were also made of silver, their shapes often echoing those created by potters in their own ruder material.

Our knowledge of table silver used during the Middle Ages is extremely limited. Many of the pieces that survive today were religious vessels or reliquaries; presumably their institutional purpose and public setting secured them greater safety than the silver objects that graced the private tables of the upper classes. Household inventories from the late medieval period offer tantalizing glimpses of the types of silver that may have been commonly used at aristocratic tables, and woodcuts of the period confirm the importance of finely crafted vessels, especially for drinking.

By the sixteenth century the range of vessels used for dining and drinking began to grow in number and complexity. Whereas the church had served as a primary patron of silversmiths and goldsmiths during the Middle Ages, the artisan's income during the period of the Renaissance derived more and more from rich and powerful secular clients. From the sixteenth century on it is possible to trace in detail a continuous development of table silver, especially in England. The most far-reaching developments came in the later part of the seventeenth and early eighteenth centuries, the first period well represented in the Chrysler collection. France during this time maintained a position of influential supremacy in the visual arts, a phenomenon both symbolized and perpetuated by Louis XIV. The court of the Sun King at Versailles was the epitome of refinement and ceremony: architecture, garden design, and furniture reflected the splendor of the king, as did the etiquette of dining and the objects that enhanced the royal table.

The royalty and aristocracy of Europe strove to emulate the style of the French court, and along with gilded furniture, rich fabrics, and virtuoso silver came new refinements for the table—specific forms for the purposes of service, such as platters, sauceboats, casters, and baskets. Many of these French forms became quite popular throughout Europe in the eighteenth century, especially in London, one of the most active and prolific centers for the production of domestic silver; it is

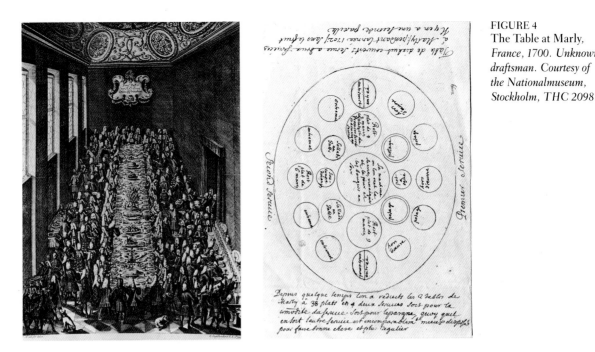

therefore not surprising that a majority of the pieces found in the Chrysler collection were made by London silversmiths.

One of the most important influences over the development of service forms was the practice of serving meals *à la française,* or in the French manner. Multiple dishes filled with a variety of foods were placed en masse on the table before the guests, creating an often bewildering array of delicacies. Such complex and theatrical service required that the table be arranged according to a careful "floor plan," often drawn up in advance by a court-appointed "architect" of the table. The ritualized service, along with the fact that such table arrangements were almost always composed with an eye toward symmetry and balance in the distribution of dishes, required an immense amount of silver. Since food was not passed in a succession of courses, individual guests presumably had ready access to dishes closest to their assigned places. Refinements in the form of small baskets, sauceboats, and condiment containers also appeared in increasing numbers on the eighteenth-century table.

Placed at intervals on the table, eighteenth-century English tablewares included platters, salvers, and small trays especially useful for holding prepared dishes (nos. 13–15). By the middle decades of the eighteenth century, such dishes followed a standard form: a flat or shallow concave center was surrounded by a raised border composed of repeated decorative motifs such as shells and gadroons. In some instances the central depression was deep enough to catch and hold any liquids that might escape from meat, fowl, or fish. Similarly designed individual silver plates were set before each guest to mark their place and to hold their portions; even today individual service plates are often placed at table prior to the seating of the guests, even though these are most often replaced with other dishes when the service begins. Many of these eighteenth-century pieces were engraved with the coat of arms or crest of the family, a clear reminder that they were meant for display as well as for use.

FIGURE 5
Design for a silver table set, Rome, Italy, 1800–1825. Pietro Belli (1780–1828). Courtesy of the Cooper-Hewitt Museum, Smithsonian Institution/Art Resource, New York; Friends of the Museum Fund, 1938-88-657.

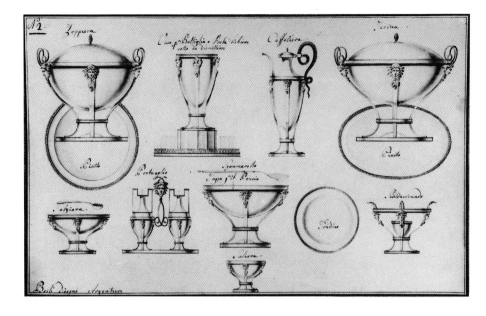

Highly practical designs such as these were supplemented at the eighteenth-century table by new and specialized forms that arose in response to the growing sophistication of table manners and food service. Among the most delightful and popular were skillfully crafted containers for various sauces. Generally oval or boat-shaped, sauceboats were equipped with an easily grasped handle and an elongated pouring lip. A London-made pair of examples from mid-century (no. 18), each supported on three cast scroll-and-shell legs, is typical of the most popular form. Ready access to sauces and condiments was especially important, so multiple sauce containers would be expected at a well-stocked table. A variation on this form, equipped with a central loop handle and two pouring lips, enabled two diners to share a single vessel (no. 17). Sauceboats remained popular throughout the eighteenth century, even as they evolved to reflect new stylistic trends. For example, a French sauceboat of the early nineteenth century (no. 19) reveals the influence of neoclassical design in its simplicity and clarity: the graceful ovoid body is supported on a central base that follows the shape of the body, and a high arched handle terminates in a dignified eagle's head. Today the descendant of these sauce containers is seen in the gravy boat that makes such a useful accompaniment to a Sunday dinner.

Another refinement for the table that gained immense popularity in the late seventeenth and eighteenth centuries was the caster (no. 20). Casters were often made in sets of three for various spices, condiments, or sugar. Larger casters were especially useful for sprinkling coarsely pulverized sugar. The apertures in the covers of most eighteenth-century casters are larger than might be expected, since at this time sugar was not sold in granulated form but was purchased in solid cones and crushed at home.

A delightful new form popularized in the 1700s was the highly ornamental silver basket, probably used for pastries or fruits. A fine example in the Chrysler Museum collection is marked by George Methuen of

London, dated 1743–44 (no. 21). Designed with bold paw-and-ball feet and an everted rim with lively ornamentation, the piece is so finely pierced that it looks like silver lace. The specialization of design forms, stimulated by rapid growth in the eighteenth-century silver market, is a trend that continued up to the present day; in the nineteenth century, for example, covered silver butter dishes appeared (no. 22), along with a variety of distinctive dishes and bowls (no. 23). By the twentieth century even children were entitled to their own special designs (no. 24).

One of the largest and most imposing objects inhabiting the dining tables of the eighteenth century was the tureen. Tureens were used primarily for serving soups, but others of similar shape may also have been used for prepared dishes such as stews or ragouts. The form is probably derived from large covered dishes used in France in the seventeenth century. Its size alone commanded attention at the table, and it was an indispensable item for the service of a grand dinner with numerous guests. The five tureens in the Chrysler Museum collection span over a century of design and a variety of styles (nos. 9–12). In the purity and simplicity of its shape and decoration, a neoclassical tureen from Europe (no. 10) stands in contrast to the boldly sculptural examples made in the nineteenth century by American silver manufacturers such as Ball, Black and Company of New York (no. 11). A return to simple and undecorated form is documented in a tureen and stand from around 1925 (no. 12).

In the French manner of service, serving dishes needed to be positioned close enough to each guest for them to be accessible. Their placement around the periphery of the table, to accommodate the diners, created a void in the table's center. This space was soon filled by increasingly elaborate centerpieces. Ornamental centerpieces, not only of silver, flourished in the seventeenth and eighteenth centuries. Assembled from a variety of materials ranging from sugar sculpture to porcelain figures, the centerpiece came to receive a great deal of attention. French centerpieces of the seventeenth century often contained a central basket or plateau, surrounded by containers for condiments and spices, and were sometimes fitted with candleholders to increase the amount of light available to the diners.

An exuberant development of these French centerpieces, the epergne became popular in elegant dining rooms in eighteenth-century England. The epergne was an ideal solution to the problems of both function and display. Used to hold a variety of attractive sweets and delicacies, these large and often extremely ornate forms dramatically defined the center of the table and assumed truly architectural significance. Most English epergnes from the middle decades of the century were constructed with four legs that supported a flower-festooned apron and a pierced central basket on an elongated column. The basic structure was surrounded by a series of attenuated scrolled arms holding aloft various baskets and dishes that could be reached easily from almost any place at the table.

By the nineteenth century an important change in dining practices had gained general acceptance: the service *à la française* of the seventeenth and eighteenth centuries was rendered outmoded by the more comfortable and accommodating service *à la russe*. According to this new ritual, prepared dishes were no longer placed on the table simultaneously. Instead, the meal was staged in successive courses; most dishes were prepared for individual servings and presented to guests in a predetermined order. Now all guests shared the same food at the same time, and the modern meal of set courses—from soup to dessert—became the preferred system of service throughout Europe.

Even with this change in service, the center of the table still held a place of importance, and the single grand epergne began to be supplemented by matching compotes or smaller footed dishes, bowls, and baskets, arranged symmetrically down the length of the table. Quite often such compotes were used for ornamental arrangements of fruit, although they could also be called into service to hold flowers, by far the most popular of nineteenth-century table decorations. The Chrysler Museum collection contains several descendants of the eighteenth-century epergne (nos. 2–4). The nineteenth-century compote, a shallow concave dish supported on a central stem, has another antecedent beyond the epergne: the form was probably derived from the sixteenth-century *tazza*, a shallow bowl supported on a tall stem, used for drinking or for display. The compote appeared in many guises during the course of the nineteenth century, sometimes with highly sculptural, figural stems or with stands that resembled three-legged Roman lamps (no. 3). Some compotes were even ornamented with stylized heads derived from Egyptian sculpture (no. 4). By the end of the century a well-stocked table would also include smaller compotes for serving sweets. The Chrysler collection's pair of footed dishes made by Gorham of Providence, Rhode Island (no. 5), shows the lush, organic decoration typical of the period. By the twentieth century compotes were deemed old fashioned, but the need for an attractive and useful container for fruits or sweets survived. Among the later objects in the Chrysler collection is a sleek and modern fruit bowl (no. 8) produced by Tiffany and Company of New York, which demonstrates that styles in silver have changed more rapidly than the functional requirements of the table.

A final flowering of the epergne form and one of this collection's most dramatic pieces is a massive and memorable centerpiece made by Gorham (no. 6). Even in the eighteenth century the epergne was an ideal choice of form for the virtuoso silversmith, and such a form was chosen by Gorham for one of the star works in their display at the 1904 St. Louis Exposition. This rare example of American silver is rendered additionally useful for the table by a pierced inset for the central basket to hold fresh flowers.

An extraordinary twentieth-century centerpiece made in Paris by Jean Puiforcat (no. 7) served as an ice-skating trophy. Only distantly related to the epergnes and compotes that preceded it, this work denies practical function; even the central bowl on a stand has been filled to overflowing with rock-crystal "ice." In its drama and presence, however, this centerpiece may be our twentieth-century equivalent of the grand displays of silver on the seventeenth-century table.

Another family of silver objects made for the table is the drinking vessel—goblets, cups, beakers, jugs, and ewers. From the earliest days of silversmithing, silver vessels for drinking were held in special regard. Wine has played an important role in many rituals, and vessels made for ceremonial use were especially prized. Although not strictly considered furnishings for the table, three ceremonial wine vessels have been included in this volume: a covered Communion cup made in London in the late sixteenth century (no. 25), fitted with a cover that can be reversed and used as a paten to hold the Eucharist; an octagonal stemmed cup made in eighteenth-century Augsburg and used as a kiddush cup (no. 26); and a simple stemmed chalice similar in form to glass vessels made in the same period, which was, according to its inscription, "Presented to the Suffolk Street Chapel by Sarah Blake" (no. 27).

Silver drinking vessels made specifically for domestic use are well known from the Middle Ages. By the eighteenth century, however, light, transparent, and fragile glass had become the preferred material for table use; when nineteenth-century mass-production techniques made glassware available to virtually everyone, silver vessels for drinking became a rarity.

Although stemmed goblets made of glass dominated the eighteenth-century table, impressive examples in silver exist, such as one made in Moscow in 1747 (no. 36). Its tapered body covered with a cage of fully pierced, lacelike silver, this goblet carries the symbolic association of chalice into the domestic context. In our own day, silver wine goblets are rarely used, although novelties such as stemmed cocktail goblets (no. 37) are curious survivals of the tradition.

The Chrysler collection includes several beakers or silver drinking vessels that would have been proud additions to the tables of the well-to-do in the sixteenth and seventeenth centuries. Rather simple, flat-based beakers were extremely popular (no. 34), many engraved with delicate ornament. Some eighteenth-century beakers, more imposing with their rococo ornamentation, were probably intended for ceremonial use or for display (no. 35), particularly when the family arms were boldly emblazoned on the surface. Simple one-handled drinking vessels such as canns, mugs, and tankards (nos. 28–33) were closely identified with everyday domestic use in the eighteenth century. The earliest of such drinking vessels in the Chrysler Museum collection is a small mug made in London in 1703–4 (no. 28), ornamented with chased flutes around the body. Its cylindrical form and flat base suggest its derivation from beakers, and its simple shape stands in contrast to the more elegant pear-shaped canns that followed in the middle years of the eighteenth century (nos. 29–31), popular both in England and in colonial America.

Another vessel associated with drinking in the seventeenth century is the squat covered cup with double cast handles (no. 39). This particular form of drinking vessel—especially useful for communal or ceremonial drinking due to its capacity and its paired handles—was in use as early as the fifteenth century. By the late seventeenth century the form was ubiquitous throughout Europe, England, and America. Often referred to as a "caudle" cup in which to serve a broth, the precise function of the vessel is difficult to determine; indeed, it may have been used for a wide variety of drinks.

The two-handled cup, which probably grew out of a highly functional form—the paired handles render it easy to lift and pass to another person—had, by the eighteenth century, assumed its role as an impressive display object more than as a practical vessel for drinking. The early-eighteenth-century Dublin-made cup in the Chrysler collection (no. 40), like most of the Irish cups known today, was fashioned without a cover. A splendid cup from the workshop of David Willaume II (no. 41), ornamented with unusually fine cast and applied strapwork, is typical of English cups of the first half of the eighteenth century. The influence of neoclassicism on this traditional form is documented by the two-handled cup marked by Robert Hennell of London in 1780–81 (no. 42). Since these cups were used primarily for display to proclaim the taste and status of their owners, it is not surprising to find that, with its connotations of ceremonial and celebratory drinking, the two-handled cup grew into the favored form for trophies and presentation pieces—often of impressive size and grandeur (nos. 43, 44). A splendid silver-gilt version was made by the renowned London silversmith Paul Storr in 1817–18 (no. 44) and used as a racing trophy. In a curious reversal, the basic trophy shape was used once again in the service of drinking in a massive punch bowl made around 1900 by the Gorham Manufacturing Company of Providence, Rhode Island (no. 47).

The family of forms related to the service of beverages includes a variety of jugs and ewers. Ewers, accompanied by matching basins, served an important function prior to the late seventeenth century, when forks came into general use and food was no longer eaten with the fingers. These vessels were kept ready in the dining room and carried by servants to guests at various times during the course of the meal, not for drinking but for cleansing the hands. A basin and ewer, sometimes filled with scented water, was a courteous refinement for guests in any sophisticated household. No longer necessary by the eighteenth century, ewers and basins en suite had been assigned to duty as display items on the sideboard, although ewers continued to be made for serving wine and water and became especially popular in the nineteenth century. An elaborately decorated water pitcher (no. 50) made by Samuel Kirk and Son from mid-nineteenth-century Baltimore was probably intended for water rather than wine: the repoussé decoration around the sides depicts a water fountain set in a lush landscape. A clever integration of ornament and purpose is typical of nineteenth-century design. This concept is delightfully expressed in a water pitcher made around 1900 and marked by Bailey, Banks, and Biddle Company of Philadelphia (no. 51). The generously curved body, applied with ornament inspired by water plants, features a large sheaf of cattails that follows the curved handle to join the lip.

A claret jug of the late nineteenth century (no. 49) embodies the interaction of two different crafts: the neck (with its classical griffins), handle, and base are made of silver, but the body is of brilliant glass, cut

FIGURE 6
New York City—The
Annual Ball and Banquet
of the Société Culinaire
Philanthropique, *c. 1870.*
Unknown draftsman.
Courtesy of the Cooper-
Hewitt Museum,
Smithsonian Institution/Art
Resource, New York; The
Kubler Collection, 3047.

in strict upright flutes—a felicitous combination, since rich red wine would be revealed jewel-like in its silver setting.

Other vessels that added special elegance to the pleasures of drinking include large punch bowls (no. 47) and wine coolers (no. 45). Even when not used on the table, such imposing objects maintained their value as display items.

Beyond the innovation and multiplication of forms that arose in response to new needs at the table, and beyond the traditional significance of silver for display, objects for the table also record the progressive interaction of the shifting cultural fashions, social customs, and economic forces that occurred between the eighteenth century and the present day. One of the most obvious and richly documented stories can be traced through the evolution of forms related to the service of tea and coffee.

Both tea and coffee were introduced to Europe during the seventeenth century and gained acceptance among a select group of aficionados who appreciated and were able to afford these curious luxuries. By the eighteenth century these beverages had come into everyday use by a wide cross section of society. The need for appropriate vessels in which to prepare and serve these drinks stimulated the production of both ceramics and silver. Thousands of teapots were made during the eighteenth century, in both earthenware and porcelain; silver, however, always maintained a position of great distinction in drawing rooms and on tea tables. Silversmiths in cities from Lisbon to London were called upon to supply the demands of a rapidly expanding market of tea and coffee drinkers. Concurrent with the growth in popularity of the drinks was an increase in the number of people who could afford to own silver for the table. From a sociological point of view, the history of silver, especially in eighteenth-century England, documents the rapid adoption of these two drinks by the general population, as well as the growing industrialization of the silver industry and the intensification of competition within the marketplace for silver and other decorative arts.

Basic shapes were well established by the early eighteenth century: coffeepots tended to be cylindrical or pear-shaped and rather tall (no. 53), while teapots sported a squatter, more globular form (no. 52). Pots were not alone on the tables of eighteenth-century caffeine addicts, however. An extended family of objects appeared in the early days of tea drinking, ranging from caddies or cannisters to store the dried leaves to a wide variety of sugar bowls and cream or milk jugs. Some silversmiths even began to specialize in tea-drinking paraphernalia during the eighteenth century, as evidenced by the Chrysler collection's pair of tea caddies (for green and black tea) made by Samuel Taylor (no. 79), exuberantly decorated with chased scrolls and blossoms. From the number of tea caddies and sugar bowls that exist today bearing Taylor's mark, we can conclude that these objects probably comprised the bulk of his shop's output.

Like tea caddies, containers for milk or cream were made in astonishing numbers throughout the eighteenth century, both in England and in America. Following the same stylistic development as the teapot, mid-century jugs were most often pear-shaped, with either three scrolled legs (no. 63) or a circular foot (no. 64). Under the influence of neoclassical fashions in the latter decades of the eighteenth century, milk jugs and sugar bowls tended to reflect the simpler and more stable shapes of classical ceramics; many cream jugs were made with little ornament, the attention focusing instead on the profile of their elegant "helmet" shapes (nos. 65–67).

A large urn became a useful addition to any eighteenth-century assemblage of tea and coffee vessels, used perhaps for serving coffee to large numbers of guest, or, more probably, to assure a constant supply of hot water to replenish the teapot. Most urns from the late eighteenth century, such as the example by James Young of London (no. 76), followed the form of the two-handled cup, which, as we have seen, was a prime candidate for dramatic display.

By the second half of the eighteenth century many people began to acquire matched sets for tea and coffee drinking. Earlier in the century a well-to-do household might have used and displayed with pride a set that contained all of the necessary utensils—from caddies and kettles to tea scoops and waste bowls—assembled from various makers and not necessarily matching exactly in decoration. Carefully matched services became more and more common toward the end of the century; by the early nineteenth century, completely matched services were de rigueur for any elegant drawing or dining room (no. 55). They continue to be the ideal in our own century (nos. 61, 62).

A significant development in the production of silver for the late-eighteenth-century domestic market involved new techniques for manu-

FIGURE 7
Aestas (*Summer*), *from* Unterschiedlich Augspurgische, *Augsburg, Germany, 1721–40. Georg Heinrich Schifflin (1666–1745) after Abraham Drentwett (1647–1727). Courtesy of the Cooper-Hewitt Museum, Smithsonian Institution/Art Resource, New York; Purchase in Memory of Mrs. J.F.K. Duer, 1962-198-32.*

facturing tea and coffee services. By the end of the century a large number of services were made of extremely thin silver, whereas teapots and coffeepots from earlier in the century tended to be weighty and substantial. A growing number of middle-class purchasers of silver stimulated competition among the silversmiths, and one way to undercut the competition was to reduce the amount of silver used in the fabrication of individual pieces. Silversmiths began using commercially rolled sheets of silver that eliminated the expense of hammering ingots into sheet prior to raising the form with hammer and anvil. The simplified forms they created —often based on geometric shapes such as ovals or cylinders—could be fabricated quickly and rather cheaply by shaping a segment of prerolled silver and soldering the seam to create a cylinder. Such designs, less expensive due to the reduced costs of material and labor, were also entirely consistent with neoclassical dictums of simplicity. Decoration on neoclassical forms also tended to reduce the amount of handwork involved: although some objects continued to be chased by hand (no. 68), a majority depended entirely on shallow, repetitive engraved designs (no. 69).

In addition to the competition brought by an expanding market of potential clients, silversmiths began to feel the economic pressure created by the growing silver-plate industry. Large firms such as those in Sheffield could offer surprisingly affordable "silver" that was actually a rather thick sheet of copper overlaid with a thin sheet of silver. When formed into a teapot or hot-water jug, however, it gave the impression of sterling.

It should also be noted that during the late eighteenth and early nineteenth centuries silver manufacturers were competing with the burgeoning ceramics and glass companies, which made the most of industrialized production methods. By the early nineteenth century the glass industry supplied most of the drinking vessels used at table, and cheap but attractive ceramics were within the budget of nearly everyone. To capitalize on this growing market of consumers, the glass industry expanded its range of forms for drinking. Whereas wine glasses had served for a variety of drinks in the eighteenth century, by the nineteenth century coordinated services were offered, each size and design specifically earmarked for a special wine—red, white, sherry, port, or champagne. Silversmiths responded in kind: by the mid-nineteenth century the multipurpose serving dish had spawned a large family of highly specialized serving dishes for game, meat, fish, fowl, and vegetables, a phenomenon that can be traced through trade catalogues issued in the course of the century.

Many silversmiths fell victim to the competitive pressures unleashed by these market forces and new technologies; others adapted by producing wares for the highly successful retailers who were able to maintain showrooms in major cities. Fewer and fewer pieces were made in small workshops on special orders for individual clients, and the large and efficient factories able to make use of mass-production methods and assembly-line techniques emerged the victors. Even as early as the late eighteenth century, British silversmith Paul Storr had been able to establish a successful "mass-production" workshop that offered a wide range of domestic silver,

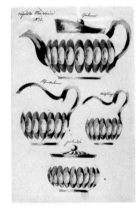

FIGURE 8
Design for a teapot, hotwater pitcher, milk pitcher, and sugar bowl, Silesia, Austria, c. 1825. Unknown designer. Courtesy of the Cooper-Hewitt Museum, Smithsonian Institution/Art Resource, New York; Friends of the Museum Fund, 1938-88-735.

ranging from butter dishes to tureens. By the early years of the nineteenth century Storr was supplying wrought silver to Rundell and Bridge, one of the largest and most successful firms operating in London. In the United States the growth of large mass-production firms was especially pronounced. The Gorham Manufacturing Company of Providence, Rhode Island, and the New York firms of Ball, Black and Company and Tiffany and Company supplied table silver to markets throughout the country; tea and coffee services were among their most popular items.

Tea and coffee services made in the nineteenth century may be read like art-historical texts, for they rapidly reflected current fashions, trends, and tastes in form and decoration. Out of the neoclassical traditions of the eighteenth century arose services that expressed the grandeur and substance of classical design, even when they were made of very thin silver, such as the teapot by Fletcher and Gardiner of Philadelphia (no. 56). Ball, Black and Company fashioned tea services with finials in the shape of classical helmets (no. 58), and some designs, such as that for a teakettle on a stand from Tiffany and Company (no. 77), are strikingly simple and modern in appearance.

By the nineteenth century silver for the table was enjoyed by more people of different economic classes than ever before. Prices for silver declined during the century, in part due to the enormous increase in silver ore coming from American silver mines in the West. As entertaining took on increasing social importance for the middle classes, the popularity of silver widened. And with the appearance of sophisticated and knowledgeable collectors of antique silver, objects that had been considered old-fashioned heirlooms took on an entirely new value. Silver for the table remained a mark of distinction; a table set with antique silver became one of special merit.

The French gastronome Jean Brillat-Savarin, writing in the early part of the nineteenth century, made a clear distinction between eating and dining. In his *Physiology of Taste or Meditations on Transcendental Gastronomy* of 1825 he contrasted the physical gratification of the appetite with the spiritual, intellectual, and fundamentally civilizing process of dining: "The pleasures of the table are known only to the human race," he declared. The preparation, presentation, and enjoyment of a meal are given value through the manner in which they are accomplished; the table is a landscape of our imagination appreciated by the intellect as well as the senses.

Silver for the table, as documented by the Chrysler Museum collection, offers a richly varied menu of social, economic, and culinary history. Silver has served many needs over the years, and it continues today to exert the magical and impressive power that has captivated our imaginations for centuries.

1

5

6

11

21

24

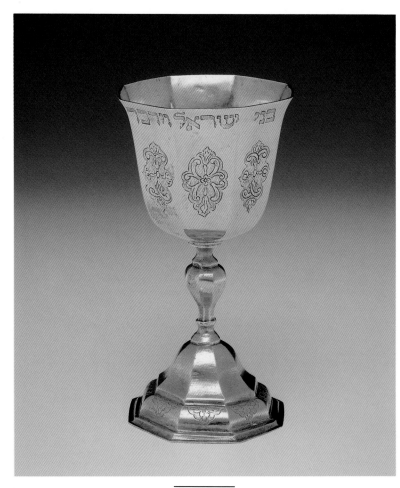

26

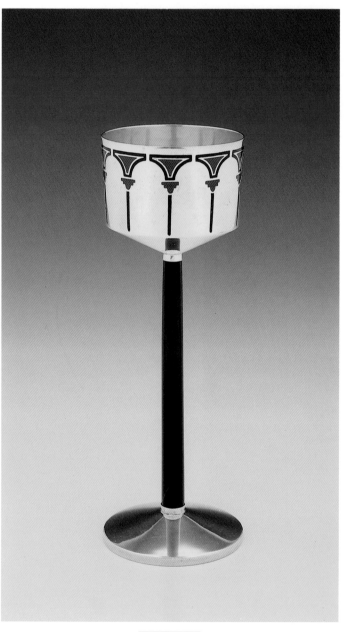

36

37

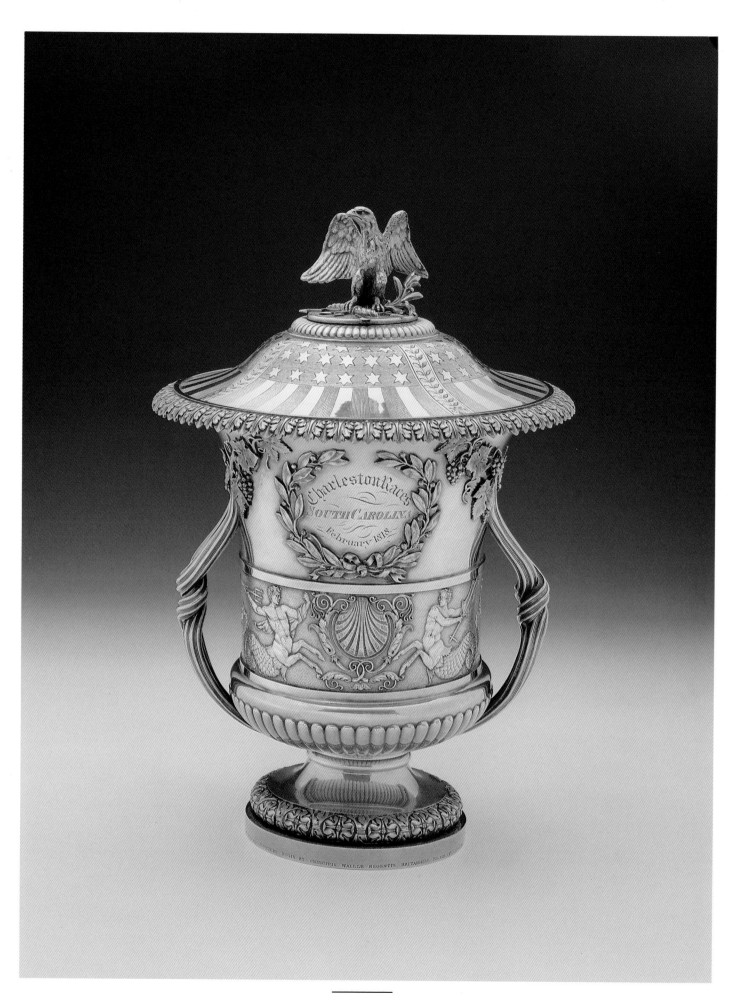

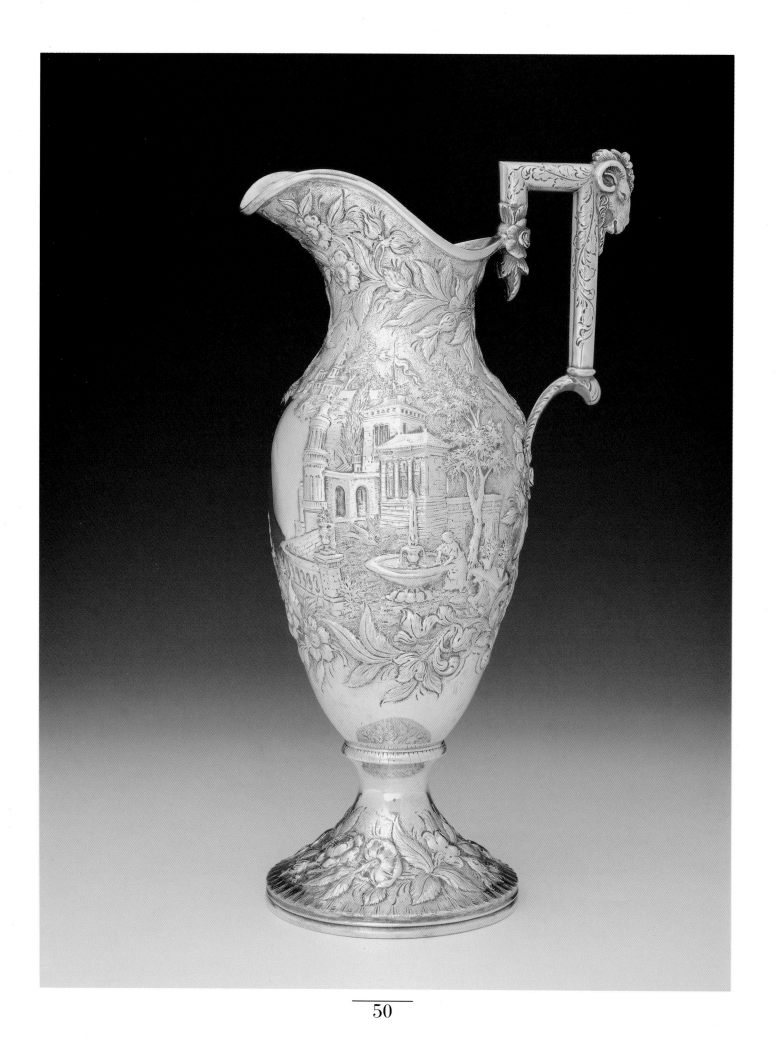

53

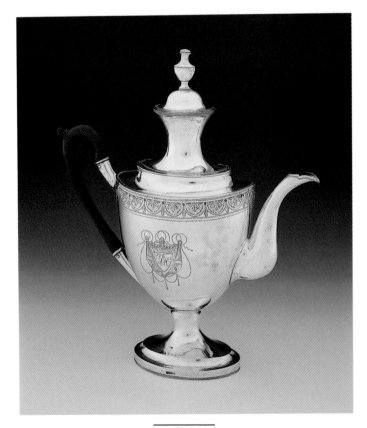

54

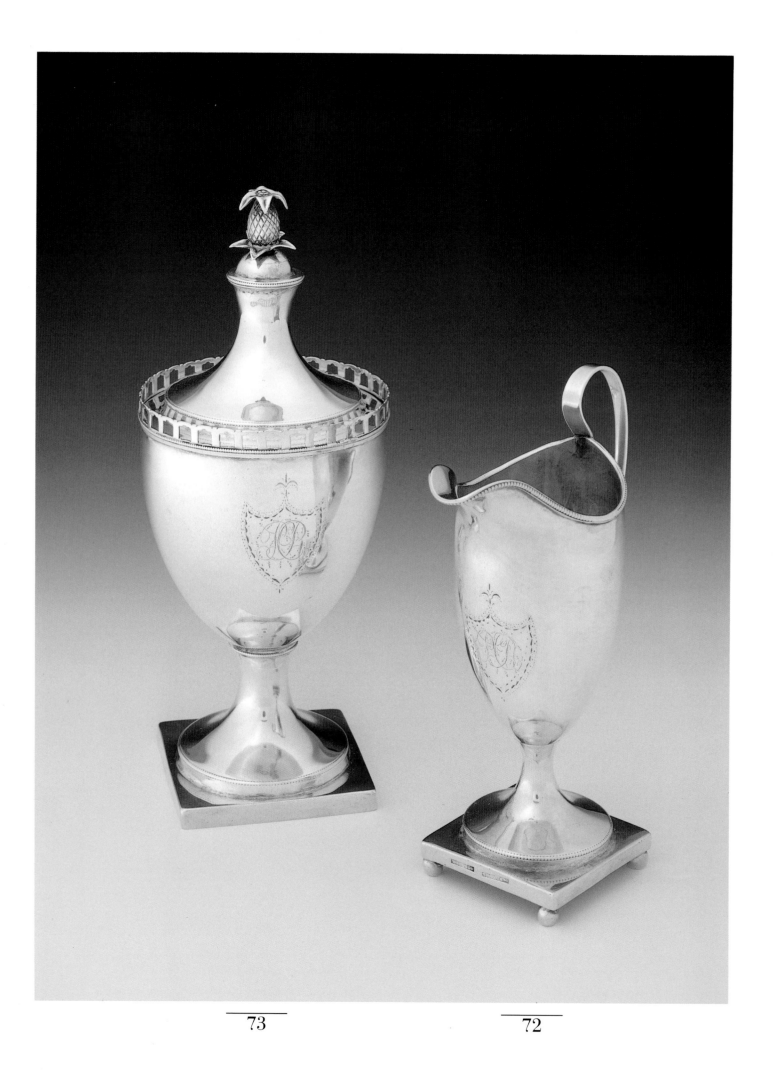

73   72

Treasures
for the Table

The Architecture
of the Table:
Centerpieces,
Compotes, and Epergnes

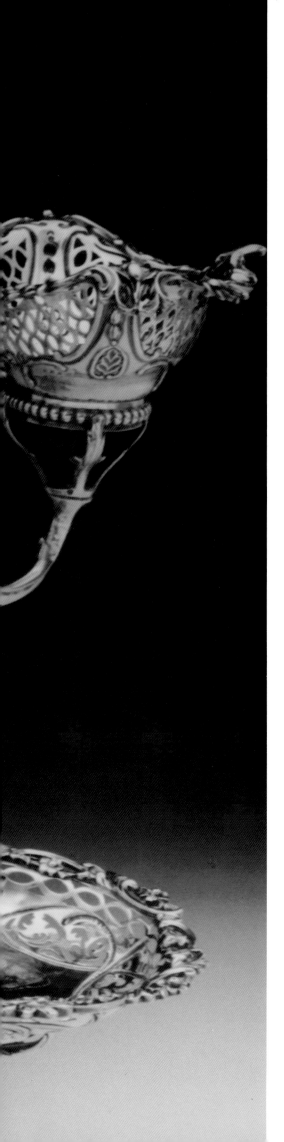

*I*mpressive in size and decoration, centerpieces, compotes, and epergnes are the most architectural of table ornaments. By the middle of the eighteenth century in England, epergnes, sometimes referred to in contemporary documents as "machines," served as the focal point in the arrangement of the table. Epergnes naturally assumed multiple functions; in the eighteenth century some were fitted with casters and candlesticks as well as a number of baskets or dishes. Nearly all were made with a large central basket, presumably for arrangements of fruit.

Although epergnes in the eighteenth century were sometimes made with separate footed dishes or baskets arranged around the central section, the tendency toward multiple parts is most clearly evident in the nineteenth century. By the middle decades of the 1800s decorations for the center of the table were often composed of a tall footed bowl accompanied by two or more smaller compotes. Such arrangements appear often in nineteenth-century depictions of dining tables, the compotes filled with pyramids of fruit or colorful arrangements of flowers.

By the beginning of the twentieth century such complex and expensive architectural embellishments were less common on the table, but the drama of the form was exploited in the development of grand display pieces, such as a massive centerpiece made by Gorham and Company of Providence, Rhode Island (no. 2).

From the seventeenth century to the present day, silversmiths have supplied a wide variety of decoratively impressive designs for the table. Centerpieces, epergnes, and compotes contributed graceful and often magnificent profiles to tables set with myriad plates, dishes, and bowls, and they certainly enjoy a special place in defining the architecture of the dining room.

1

George III epergne

LONDON, ENGLAND, 1770–71
PRODUCED BY THOMAS PITTS I
H 16 in. (40.6 cm), L 26 in. (66.0 cm),
W 21 in. (53.3 cm)
78.116a–n

Hallmarks: Central support (78.116a, struck on side where top bowl fits): Black letter capital P (date letter for 1770–71); Leopard head crowned (London assay); Lion passant (sterling standard); T P (maker's mark). Large basket (78.116b, struck on bottom): Marked the same as the central support with engraved 158=17. Pair of small baskets (78.116c–d, struck on bottom): Lion passant (sterling standard); T P (maker's mark). Set of four dishes (78.116e–h, struck on bottom): Marked the same as the small baskets. Arm supports for two small baskets (78.116i–j, not marked). Arm supports for four dishes (78.116k–n, not marked).

This high-rococo–style epergne was developed for use in the center of the table so that guests could help themselves to sweetmeats, fruits, and other desserts placed in its baskets and dishes. It is not known when the epergne form was first developed, but most of them date from the middle of the eighteenth century on. There has been much confusion as to the "T P" maker's mark on this piece. It has been attributed to Thomas Pitts, Thomas Powell, and others, but recent research has made it fairly certain that this mark belongs to Thomas Pitts I, who specialized in making epergnes. It would originally have had a specially fitted case that is no longer with it. The epergne is engraved with unidentified arms and crest.

2

Renaissance revival centerpiece or fruit dish

PROVIDENCE, RHODE ISLAND, C. 1863–65
PRODUCED BY GORHAM AND COMPANY
H 12 in. (30.5 cm), D 11 in. (27.9 cm)
77.499

Hallmarks (struck on bottom): Clark and Biddle (retailers); 425 (design number); Lion (silver); Anchor (symbol of Rhode Island); Sterling (silver standard); B2 (perhaps a workman's mark).

Centerpieces of this type were used on sideboards and in the center of the dining table. They were in great demand, especially during the last quarter of the nineteenth century when the Renaissance revival style was popular. Designs of this type were termed "neo grec" by French design books of the period, although "Victorian Renaissance" is the term more commonly used today.

3

Medallion compote

PROVIDENCE, RHODE ISLAND, C. 1863–65
DESIGNED BY GEORGE WILKINSON (1819–94)
PRODUCED BY GORHAM AND COMPANY
H 9⅝ in. (24.5 cm), L 11¾ in. (29.8 cm),
W 8 in. (20.3 cm)
77.537

Hallmarks (struck on bottom): STARR & MARCUS (New York retailer); Lion (silver); Anchor (symbol of Rhode Island); G (for Gorham); 290 (pattern number).

The medallion pattern, which featured classical heads in medallions, was one of Gorham's most popular designs. The Greek-key border along its shaped edge repeats the classical motif.

4

Centerpiece or fruit dish

NEW YORK, NEW YORK, C. 1865–70
PRODUCED BY BALL, BLACK AND COMPANY
H 13 in. (33.0 cm), D 10⅝ in. (27.0 cm)
77.506

Hallmarks (struck on bottom): BALL, BLACK & CO. (manufacturing company); NEW YORK (place of manufacture); ENGLISH SILVER (sterling standard).

Around 1870 a number of silver manufacturers, including Gorham Manufacturing Company, turned out work in the Egyptian revival style. This centerpiece's cast heads of Egyptian pharaohs place it within that period. The design may have been inspired by French Empire furniture mounts commemorating Napoleon's Egyptian campaign earlier in the century. The bowl is engraved with vines and leaves forming a reserve with the conjoined initials CB.

1

2

3

4

Pair of Martelé footed dishes

PROVIDENCE, RHODE ISLAND, 1899
DESIGNED BY WILLIAM C. CODMAN (1839–1921)
PRODUCED BY
GORHAM MANUFACTURING COMPANY
H 5½ in. (14.0 cm), D 12¼ in. (31.1 cm)
71.951a–b

Hallmarks (struck inside pedestal foot): Lion (silver); Eagle over an anchor (symbol of Rhode Island); 950-1000 fine, encircled (quality of silver); + (unknown); Sickle (mark for year 1899).

The first pieces of a line Gorham called Martelé (the French word for hand-hammered) were introduced in New York at the Waldorf Astoria Hotel in November 1897. Production had begun a year earlier, after Gorham's workmen were trained in the old method of hand raising a piece from a block of silver (as opposed to using a machine). Martelé objects were exhibited in this country and abroad, but no sales were made until 1899 or 1900. This pair of footed dishes is unique, as indicated by the encircled 950-1000 mark, which was used for custom orders only. The dishes were probably used for serving bonbons. They are in the art nouveau style that reached its height in France around 1900. Artists and craftsmen working in the art nouveau style drew their inspiration from nature, stylizing and twisting plants, flowers, and human figures into decorative designs. The undulating border and the chasing of the leafage, which forms reserves with a child's head, are very much in the art nouveau idiom. The centers are plain except for the engraved conjoined initials FA.

6

Martelé centerpiece

PROVIDENCE, RHODE ISLAND, 1904
DESIGNED BY WILLIAM CHRISTMAS CODMAN
(1839–1921)
SILVERSMITH, WILLIAM (TED) CODMAN
PRODUCED BY
GORHAM MANUFACTURING COMPANY
H 22½ in. (57.2 cm), L 35 in. (88.9 cm),
W 22 in. (55.9 cm)
78.128a–g

Hallmarks: Main support (78.128a, struck on bottom): Martelé (name of the line); Lion (silver); Eagle over an anchor (symbol of Rhode Island); G (for Gorham); 950-1000 fine (grade of silver); FFK (model). Four dishes fitting into arms (78.128b–e, struck on bottom of each): 950-1000 fine (grade of silver); Roman capital A and rubbed out number 3005 (number added by mistake); FFK (model). Large central dish (78.128f, struck on bottom): Marked the same as the four dishes from arms. Flower holder fitting into central dish (78.128g, silver gilt with no space for marking): Unmarked.

This centerpiece is finely chased with art nouveau designs, and the handles of its main bowl are formed of cast and applied figures of mermaids. Placed in the central support is the cast figure of a winged woman and four whiplash arms, which support the four smaller bowls and have at their bases the face of a woman with long flowing hair. Four dishes extend out from the central support at its base. It has long been thought that this centerpiece was made for Gorham's Martelé exhibit at the St. Louis Exposition of 1904, where their silver display won every gold medal for its division. Charles H. Carpenter, Jr.'s 1982 book on Gorham silver indicates that pieces made for the Exposition were marked with a capital "T" with a lower-case "s" imposed over it. The centerpiece does not contain this mark, but Edward Money of Gorham's design department has learned that the centerpiece was indeed made for the Exposition. Gorham's files contain a photograph of the piece and records indicating that it was begun on January 5, 1904, with an estimated 73 hours of working time by Ted Codman, son of the chief designer, and the projected use of 390.8 ounces of silver. The actual amount of silver used and the time for labor are also recorded as follows: 392 ounces of silver; chasing, 532 hours; making time, 425 hours; casting, 25½ hours; turning, 2 hours. The total cost of the centerpiece was $1,600—a large sum of money at a time when the hourly wage for silversmiths was 50¢ per hour.

7

Trophy/centerpiece

PARIS, FRANCE, C. 1923
DESIGNED BY JEAN PUIFORCAT (1897–1945)
H 10¾ in. (27.3 cm), D 21½ in. (54.6 cm)
78.245

Hallmarks: Jean E. Puiforcat (designer's signature engraved on silver base); Lozenge with E and P flanking image of a knife (Puiforcat's official mark struck above signature); Head of Minerva (silver standard struck above signature inside enameled rim).

Jean Puiforcat, being a sportsman, did not like the banal trophies that had been in use for so long and decided to develop a different and more exciting design. This piece, the Jean Potain figure-skating trophy for the Palais des Glaces in Paris, is surely different. It takes the form of a frozen fountain on a lapis lazuli and silver pedestal in the center of a frozen pool. The ice in the fountain and in the pool is made of rock crystal, while the surrounding balustrade is of silver and lapis lazuli. The silver panels between the lapis columns have been enameled to hide the engraved names of the winners of this trophy, thus making it useful as a centerpiece. The stepped silver base rests on a marble plinth. This must be the most elaborate work of Jean Puiforcat, who is better known for his simple silver designs.

Bowl

NEW YORK, NEW YORK, C. 1947–1956
PRODUCED BY TIFFANY AND COMPANY
H 4½ in. (11.4 cm), L 16 in. (40.6 cm),
W 8 in. (20.3 cm)
77.1064

Hallmarks (struck on bottom): TIFFANY & CO/MAKERS (manufacturing company); Sterling Silver (silver standard); 23347 (pattern number); M (initial of Louis de Bébian Moore, president of the company, 1947–55).

The graceful shape of this bowl—most likely used for fruit—and the design of its handles probably have their roots in the art deco period, around 1930. The only decoration is a chased design on the handles and the conjoined initials FJS engraved on the interior of the bowl.

6

7

8

Refinements of the Table: Sauceboats, Tureens, Baskets, Salvers, Platters, Dishes, and Casters

The increasing use of silver at table in the eighteenth century stimulated the production of a large and useful family of additional refinements to the service of a meal. Sauceboats began to appear in England in the early years of the eighteenth century. Some were made to stand alone, resting on three or four ornamental legs, while others were made with accompanying stands. Many examples from this period feature double pouring lips. Peter Archambo, whose mark appears on the pair of sauceboats of 1741–42 in the Chrysler collection (no. 17), became well known for his extensive production of tableware; numerous sauceboats bear his mark.

Soup tureens, like sauceboats, achieved popularity in the first half of the eighteenth century. Derived from large, deep covered bowls in common use at French tables by the end of the seventeenth century, the silver tureen was a mainstay of the well-furnished eighteenth-century table. Paul Storr, whose mark appears on the tureens of 1811–12 in the Chrysler collection (no. 9), headed one of the most prolific workshops active in late-eighteenth- and early-nineteenth-century London; his tureens follow a standard format— a capacious bowl supported on a central foot. Alternatively, some tureens were designed with four feet, and both types were frequently accompanied by a stand, which added to the elegance of the form.

Bread, pastry, or dessert baskets made of silver have a long history in England; examples of the form, complete with pierced sides, are known from as early as the late sixteenth century. In the eighteenth century, however, silver baskets—most often pierced in patterns that resemble wicker, latticework, or lace—became indispensable additions to the table. Either oval or round, these useful and elegant forms were made by some of the most important London silversmiths.

Salvers and dishes were among the most frequently used objects on the eighteenth-century table, ranging in size from small individual plates to large oval or round dishes for presentation and service. Their utilitarian designs, not linked to the requirements of serving any specific dish or course, made them useful at many stages in the meal. This functional flexibility has allowed silver trays and dishes to remain an important part of table service to this day.

9

Pair of George III covered soup tureens

LONDON, ENGLAND, 1811–12
PRODUCED BY PAUL STORR (1771–1844)
H 12½ in. (31.8 cm), D 11 in. (27.9 cm)
78.87a–b

Hallmarks: Cover (78.87a, struck on base of finial): King's head (duty mark); Lion passant (sterling standard); P S (maker's mark). Tureen (78.87a, struck on foot rim): P S (maker's mark); Lion passant (sterling standard); Leopard head crowned (London assay); Roman capital Q (date letter for 1811–12). Cover (78.87b, struck on base of finial and partially on flange): P S (maker's mark; on finial); King's head (duty mark; on finial); Lion passant (sterling standard; on finial and flange); Roman capital Q (date letter for 1811–12; on flange). Tureen (78.87b): Marked the same as the tureen (78.87a).

The unusual elephant-head finials resting on a coronet suggest that these tureens were quite possibly made for an Englishman who had served his country in India. The engraved coat of arms on each tureen has not been identified, however. This pair of tureens represents Paul Storr's work at its best, before the excesses of his Victorian period.

10

Covered soup tureen on stand

EUROPEAN, EARLY NINETEENTH CENTURY
PRODUCED BY DEHIO (?)
H 18 in. (45.7 cm), L 19½ in. (49.5 cm),
W 12 in. (30.5 cm)
77.619a–c

Hallmarks: Cover (77.619a, struck on rim): 13 DEHIO and a cross (unidentified). Tureen (77.619b, struck on foot rim): A cross and DEHIO (unidentified); No 2 illegible 3334 Coy, engraved very lightly on opposite side of foot (unidentified). Stand (77.619c, struck on side of base): A cross and DEHIO (unidentified); No 2 illegible 134½ Coy, engraved very lightly opposite side of base (unidentified).

This beautiful neoclassical tureen, whose marks have not been identified, bears an engraved coat of arms, also unidentified. Some design elements, such as a stamped or rolled band of vine-and-leaf decoration, suggest that it was produced in the nineteenth century.

9

10

11

Renaissance revival covered soup tureen

NEW YORK, NEW YORK, C. 1860
PRODUCED BY BALL, BLACK AND COMPANY
H 15¼ in. (38.7 cm), L 16 in. (40.6 cm),
W 11½ in. (29.2 cm)
MUSEUM PURCHASE WITH THE JACK FORKER
CHRYSLER MEMORIAL FUND 75.72.5

Hallmark (struck on bottom): BALL, BLACK & CO. (manufacturing company); NEW YORK (place of manufacture); 169 (pattern number?); ENGLISH STERLING (silver standard).

This extremely heavy high-Victorian tureen has finely cast decorations, including a woman's head with long drop earrings on each side, lion-head handles, and a recumbent lion as the finial on the cover. The lion holds a shield with the initials M/R/M.

12

Art deco covered soup tureen and stand

PARIS, FRANCE, C. 1925
PRODUCED BY TÉTARD FRÈRES
H 9½ in. (24.1 cm), L 21 in. (53.3 cm),
W 14 in. (35.6 cm)
77.1244a–c

Hallmarks: Cover (77.1244a, struck on lip): Head of Minerva (grade of silver); Lozenge with T Freres (mark of the French maker); 925 (English mark for grade of silver); Sign of the constellation Leo (English import mark for London). Tureen (77.124b): Head of Minerva (grade of silver; struck under each handle, on foot, and on side just below lip); Lozenge with T Freres (mark of the French maker; struck on foot); CJF/Ltd (mark of the English importer C. J. Vander; struck on canted corner); Sign of the constellation Leo (English import mark for London; struck on canted corner); 925 (English mark for grade of silver; struck on canted corner); K (date letter of import, 1925; struck on canted corner). Stand (77.124c): Head of Minerva (grade of silver; struck on edge of front of stand and on reverse near edge); Lozenge with T Freres (mark of the French maker; struck on bottom); CJV/Ltd (mark of the English importer C. J. Vander; struck on bottom); 925 (English mark for grade of silver; struck on bottom); K (date letter of import, 1925; struck on bottom).

The discovery of the French *poinçons* and the English import mark confirm the French origin of this ensemble, long thought to be English. Its extremely simple decoration, limited to the ivory of the finial and the canted corners, is typical of the period.

11

12

13

George II salver

LONDON, ENGLAND, 1758–59
PRODUCED BY RICHARD RUGG
H 1 in. (2.5 cm), D 6½ in. (16.5 cm)
78.108

Hallmarks (struck on bottom): Black letter capital C (date letter for 1758–59); Lion passant (sterling standard); Leopard head crowned (London assay); R R (maker's mark).

The small size of this salver suggests that it probably held a drinking vessel, and perhaps letters or calling cards at a later date. The coat of arms is unidentified.

14

Pair of George II meat dishes

LONDON, ENGLAND, 1758–59
PRODUCED BY THOMAS HEMING
H 1¾ in. (4.5 cm), L 18½ in. (47.0 cm),
W 13¼ in. (33.7 cm)
78.125a–b

Hallmarks (struck on bottom of each): Black letter capital C (date letter for 1758–59); Lion passant (sterling standard); Leopard head crowned (London assay); T H (maker's mark). Other marks: 78.125a: N 20 ″ 54 ″ 16 (inventory numbers showing the position of the pieces as part of a large service); 78.125b: N 18 ″ 57 ″ 7 (inventory numbers showing the position of the pieces as part of a large service).

These two oval dishes have shaped gadroon-and-shell edges, which are cast and applied. Their handles are formed of cast and applied shells. The coats of arms are unidentified. The delicacy and fineness of execution of these two dishes reflect the teaching of silversmith Peter Archambo, who was of French Huguenot ancestry. Thomas Heming was apprenticed to Archambo in 1738, and there is a marked French influence in his early works. Heming learned well and became an outstanding London silversmith; in 1760 he was appointed silversmith to King George III and created some of the regalia and plate for the king's coronation.

15

Pair of George II salvers

LONDON, ENGLAND, 1764–65
PRODUCED BY EBENEZER COKER (D. 1783)
H 1⅛ in. (2.9 cm), D 8 in. (20.3 cm)
78.118a–b

Hallmarks (struck on bottom of each): Black letter capital I (date letter for 1764–65); Lion passant (sterling standard); Leopard head crowned (London assay); E C (maker's mark).

These round salvers have undulating gadrooned edges finely spaced with applied shell and fanlike decorations. The center of each salver is engraved with a lion rampant, probably an unidentified crest.

16

Pair of George III dinner plates

LONDON, ENGLAND, 1767–68
PRODUCED BY WILLIAM GRUNDY
H ¾ in. (1.9 cm), D 10 in. (25.4 cm)
78.90a–b

Hallmarks (struck on bottom of each plate): Black letter capital M (date letter for 1767–68); Lion passant (sterling standard); Leopard head crowned (London assay); WG (maker's mark). Other marks (engraved on bottom of each plate): 78.90a: N 42 (number in the set of plates); H.K (unknown). 78.90b: N 45 (number in the set of plates); H.K (unknown).

These round plates have undulating gadrooned edges spaced with fanlike decorations that are cast and applied. The plates are engraved on the rim with a coat of arms containing the motto Nec Sinit Esse Feros (Nor Does He Allow to Be Savage). The arms are unidentified.

17

Pair of George II sauceboats

LONDON, ENGLAND, 1741–42
PRODUCED BY PETER ARCHAMBO I
H 8 in. (20.3 cm), L 9 in. (22.9 cm),
W 4¾ in. (12.1 cm)
78.123a–b

Hallmarks (struck on bottom of each sauceboat): Leopard head crowned (London assay); Roman small f (date letter for 1741–42); Lion passant (sterling standard); PA (maker's mark).

These double-lipped sauceboats have unusual cast and applied handles of entwined eels. The arms of Grover are engraved on each side with two mottos, Tria Juncia In Uno (Three Joined in One), the motto of the Order of the Bath, and Laudo Manente (I Praise Him Who Remains), the Grover motto.

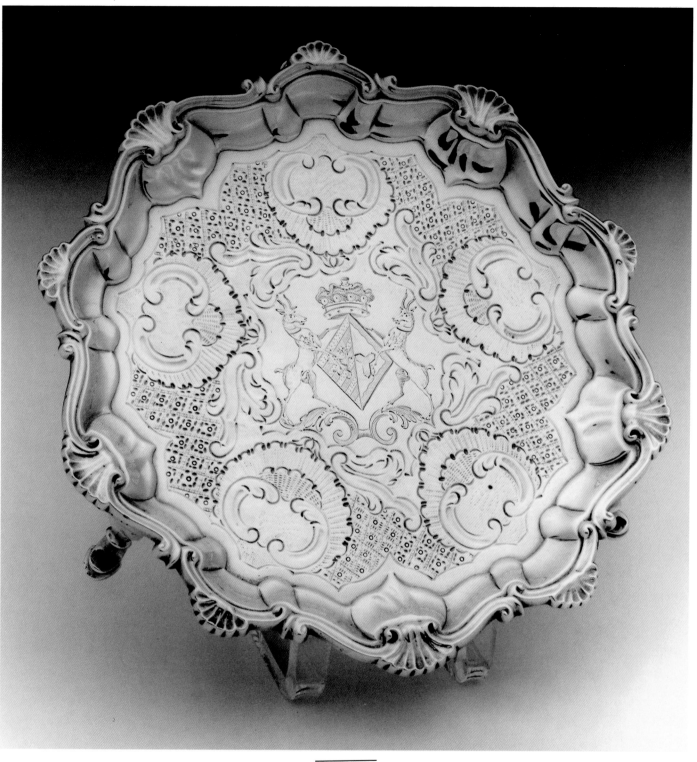

13

14

15

16

17

18

Pair of George II sauceboats

LONDON, ENGLAND, 1749–50
PRODUCED BY FULLER WHITE
H 4¾ in. (12.1 cm), L 9 in. (22.9 cm),
W 4½ in. (11.4 cm)
78.119a–b

Hallmarks (struck on bottom of each sauceboat): Leopard head crowned (London assay); Roman small o (date letter for 1749–50); FW (maker's mark); Lion passant (sterling standard).

These bulbous sauceboats are striking for their plain design, which is relieved by the elegant shaped, cast, and applied handles and the three scroll feet, headed and terminated by boldly cast shells and applied to the body.

19

Empire saucier

PARIS (?), C. 1805–15
PRODUCED BY UNIDENTIFIED MAKER
H 8½ in. (21.6 cm), L 9¾ in. (24.8 cm),
W 3⅞ in. (9.9 cm)
77.608

Hallmarks (struck on side of base and on bottom): Obliterated *poinçon*; Lozenge with a heart and a D (unidentified maker's mark).

This boat-shaped *saucier* is notable for its finely cast and applied eagle-head handle. The applied base is decorated with water leaves and beading. This *saucier* was probably inspired by Napoleon's Egyptian campaign. There should be a stand, but it is no longer with the object. An identical *saucier*, a copy made in 1880 by Odiot, was sold at Sotheby's in Monaco on May 10, 1987, lot 68.

20

Caster

LONDON, ENGLAND, 1711–12
PRODUCED BY AMBROSE STEVENSON
H 7 in. (17.8 cm), D 3 in. (7.6 cm)
78.80

Hallmarks (struck on bottom): Black letter small q (date letter for 1711–12); Figure of Britannia (sterling standard); Lion's head erased (sterling standard); AS (maker's mark).

This baluster-shaped caster has a domed and pierced cover. Casters were used for dry condiments such as sugar, salt, pepper, dry mustard, and spices. They were often made in sets of varying sizes and placed on a matching caster stand. The female figure struck on the bottom, called Britannia, was traditionally used to indicate that a higher grade of silver had been employed; this practice was short-lived, since the softer silver wore down much more quickly. The engraved crest has not been identified.

21

George II table basket

LONDON, ENGLAND, 1743–44
PRODUCED BY GEORGE METHUEN
H 11 in. (27.9 cm), L 14½ in. (36.8 cm),
W 11½ in. (29.4 cm)
78.126

Hallmarks (struck on bottom with the maker's mark stamped twice on underside of handle): G M (maker's mark); Lion passant (sterling standard); Leopard head crowned (London assay); Roman small h (date letter for 1743–44).

George Methuen's works are of such high-quality design and craftsmanship that it is strange that so little is known about him. This basket is exemplary, with its heavy weight and elaborate casting, piercing, and chasing. The swing handle has female heads with leafage facing out, and at each end of the basket are masks of bearded men. The interior has an engraved coat of arms with the motto Firm. This motto is also engraved on the handle. The coat of arms remains unidentified.

22

Renaissance revival covered butter dish

NEW YORK, NEW YORK, C. 1871
PRODUCED BY WOOD AND HUGHES
H 6¾ in. (17.2 cm), D 7 in. (17.8 cm)
83.22a–c

Hallmarks (struck on bottom): W∾H (maker's mark); 900-1000 (silver standard).

Many silver companies, including Wood and Hughes, produced vast table services in the Renaissance revival style in the late nineteenth century. This covered butter dish, with its Janus-headed finial and finely cast masks, is typical of the period. It was probably part of a service that included the pair of condiment dishes (no. 23) also in this volume.

18

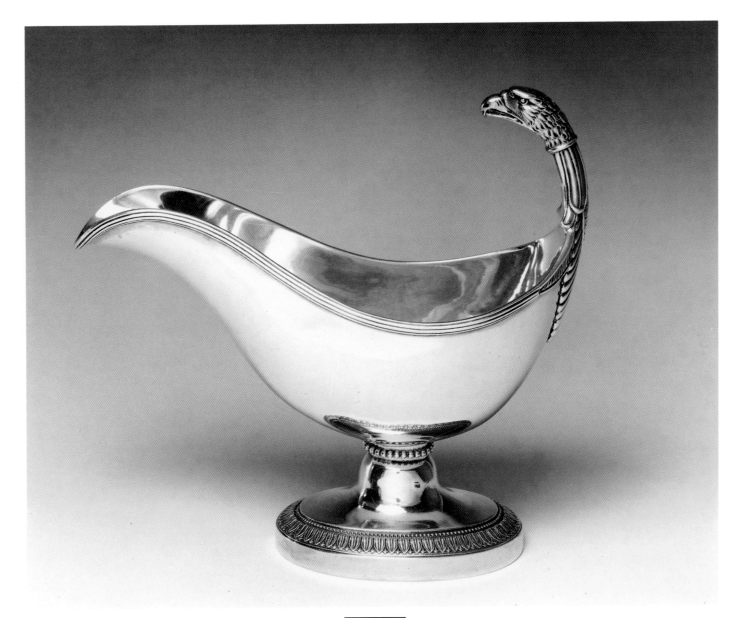

19

21

22

23

Pair of Renaissance revival condiment dishes

NEW YORK, NEW YORK, C. 1871
PRODUCED BY WOOD AND HUGHES
H 4¾ in. (12.1 cm), L 9¼ in. (23.5 cm),
W 4⅞ in. (12.4 cm)
77.503a–b

Hallmarks (struck on bottom): 77.503a: W ω H (maker's mark); 900-1000 (silver standard). 77.503b: W ω H (maker's mark); 900-1000 (silver standard).

Long catalogued as sauceboats, these dishes were actually used for condiments. They display the same design elements as the covered butter dish (no. 22) in this volume and may be part of a service. They bear the monogram JLT in script on each rim and show traces of gilding.

Child's four-piece table service

NEW YORK, NEW YORK, C. 1903
MANUFACTURED BY TIFFANY AND COMPANY
GIFT OF FRANK A. VANDERLIP, JR. 76.52.8–11

Ivory-handled porringer
H 2 in. (5.1 cm), L 8¾ in. (22.2 cm),
D 5½ in. (14.0 cm)
76.52.8

Hallmarks (struck on bottom): TIFFANY & CO. (maker's mark); 1550 2 MAKERS 5947 (pattern and order numbers); STERLING SILVER/925-1000 (silver standard); C (initial of Charles T. Cook, president of the company, 1902–7).

Plate
H ¼ in. (.6 cm), D 8 in. (20.3 cm)
76.52.9

Hallmarks (struck on bottom): TIFFANY & CO. (maker's mark); 1550 1 MAKERS 5947 (pattern and order numbers); STERLING SILVER/925-1000 (silver standard); C (initial of Charles T. Cook, president of the company, 1902–7).

Bowl
H 2½ in. (6.4 cm), D 5 in. (12.7 cm)
76.52.10

Hallmarks (struck on bottom): TIFFANY & CO. (maker's mark); 15499 MAKERS 5947 (pattern and order numbers); STERLING SILVER/925-1000 (silver standard); C (initial of Charles T. Cook, president of the company, 1902–7).

Underplate for bowl
H ½ in. (1.3 cm), D 6⅞ in. (17.5 cm)
76.52.11

Hallmarks (struck on bottom): Marked the same as the bowl.

This is a delightful service in the art nouveau style, beautifully chased with designs from nursery rhymes and fairy tales in reserves. The porringer bears a design illustrating the nursery rhyme "Tom Tom the Piper's Son"; the plate bears a design illustrating the fairy tale "Little Red Riding Hood"; and the designs on the bowl and underplate illustrate the nursery rhyme "Sing a Song of Sixpence." All except the bowl are engraved on the inside with the monogram F.A.V.Jr, and each item is engraved on the bottom with the inscription From James Stillman/April 5th 1907.

23

24

Drinking:
Ceremony
and Conviviality

The early association of wine and silver, which can be traced to the preclassical world, has secured silver drinking vessels a position of special regard. Even used in a purely domestic context, such as at the dining table, vessels made of silver or silver gilt have always combined ceremony with conviviality and pleasure.

Vessels made specifically for religious use survive from virtually all periods, although many domestic drinking vessels have disappeared. Silver was always a ready source of cash, and it was not unusual for families to melt down their silver in times of need. Domestic silver in particular also suffered from the vagaries of finance and fashion, and many drinking vessels—cups, beakers, goblets, and two-handled cups—were refashioned to update their forms and decorations. By contrast, reliquaries and ceremonial vessels were often lovingly preserved by religious institutions.

With the increasing use of glass at table during the eighteenth and nineteenth centuries, silver goblets and beakers for domestic use declined in numbers. In the eighteenth century, however, silver mugs or canns were extremely popular. The form was also favored in American colonial cities such as Boston.

Accessory pieces connected with the drinking of wine and water were made in considerable numbers, ranging from large silver wine coolers (for holding bottles of wine in chilled water) to coasters (for protecting the mahogany tabletop from stains). Large wine coolers made in the late seventeenth and early eighteenth centuries could accommodate several bottles or containers; declining in popularity in the second half of the eighteenth century, they were supplanted by wine coolers that held a single bottle. This latter form survives to the present day, most frequently used in restaurants to chill white wines.

Two-handled cups, made in sizes that encouraged shared drinking, declined in popularity as a useful form in the eighteenth century, although they continued to appear in displays of ceremonial or commemorative silver. The punch bowl designed to hold substantial amounts of mulled spiritous drinks was another ceremonial vessel. Nineteenth-century entertaining, which often included large numbers of guests at receptions and soirées, depended upon massive punch bowls, often fashioned en suite with ladles.

Ceremonial Vessels: Ecclesiastical

25

Elizabeth I Communion cup and paten

LONDON, ENGLAND, 1572–73
PRODUCED BY AB (?)
H 8⅞ in. (22.6 cm), D 4 in. (10.2 cm)
78.79a–b

Hallmarks (struck on lip of cup and top of paten): Black letter small p (date mark for 1572–73); Lion passant (sterling standard); Crowned leopard head (London assay); AB (conjoined; maker's mark —possibly Andrew Bawdyn).

Many of these cups and patens were made in the late sixteenth century, when the old Catholic chalices in almost every parish church were being replaced with Protestant Communion cups.

26

Silver-gilt kiddush cup

AUGSBURG, GERMANY, 1737–39
PRODUCED BY JOHANNES MITTNACHT III
H 5¼ in. (13.3 cm), D 2⅞ in. (7.3 cm)
77.612

Hallmarks (struck on side below lip): Pine cone over a C (mark for Augsburg 1737–39).

This silver-gilt cup is part of Jewish ritual silverware. It was used for drinking wine on special occasions such as ceremonies for religious holidays, evening meals preceding the sabbath, and weddings. The lip is inscribed in Hebrew: So Moses declared to the Israelites the set times of the Lord (Leviticus 23:44).

27

Communion cup

BOSTON, MASSACHUSETTS, C. 1805–10
PRODUCED BY ALFRED AND GEORGE WELLES
H 5¹¹⁄₁₆ in. (14.5 cm), D 3¼ in. (8.3 cm)
GIFT OF MR. AND MRS. EVERETT DURGIN 71.819

Hallmarks (struck on bottom of foot near rim): A&G.WELLES (maker's mark).

This Communion cup is a goblet originally created for domestic use. Matching cups can be found in the Clearwater collection, the Metropolitan Museum of Art, New York; and the Museum of Fine Arts, Boston. The bowl is engraved in script with the letter B and the words Presented to the/Suffolk Street Chapel /by/Sarah Blake.

25

26

Presented to the
Suffolk Street Chapel
by
Sarah Blake

27

Beakers, Goblets, Tankards, Mugs, and Canns: Secular

28

Queen Anne mug

LONDON, ENGLAND, 1703–4
PRODUCED BY WILLIAM DENNY
H 4¼ in. (10.8 cm), D 3⅞ in. (9.9 cm)
78.81

Hallmarks (struck to right of handle near lip): DE in a quatrefoil (maker's mark); Britannia (sterling standard); Lion's head erased (London assay); Court-hand G (date letter for 1703–4).

The area below the rim is chased and engraved with a raised rib. The main body of the mug has a blank cartouche, and the handle is hollow and scroll-shaped.

29

Cann

BOSTON, MASSACHUSETTS, C. 1725
PRODUCED BY JOHN BURT (1692–1745)
H 5⅜ in. (13.7 cm), D 4¼ in. (10.8 cm)
71.823

Hallmarks (struck to left side of handle near lip): JOHN/BURT (maker's mark).

This cann has a bulbous body with deeply incised paired lines below its everted rim and a cast molded foot. The cast scroll handle is hollow with a molded body drop at its upper joining. The handle has a long grip with a low vent hole, under which are the engraved initials:

A
I * M

M * A

30

George II cann

LONDON, ENGLAND, 1753–54
PRODUCED BY SAMUEL WIGHT WELLES
H 4¾ in. (12.1 cm), D 3½ in. (8.9 cm)
78.110

Hallmarks (struck on bottom): Lion passant (sterling standard); Crowned leopard head (London assay); Roman small s (date letter for 1753–54); S.W in script (maker's mark).

This cann has a bulbous body, a scroll handle, and an applied molded rim on a splayed foot that is cast and molded. Its body is engraved with an unidentified coat of arms and, below this, the name Ann Pemberton.

31

Cann

BOSTON, MASSACHUSETTS, C. 1760
PRODUCED BY BENJAMIN BURT (1729–1805)
H 5⅜ in. (14.3 cm), D 4 in. (10.2 cm)
71.818

Hallmarks: BENJAMIN/BURT (struck on bottom; maker's mark); B.BURT (struck on side under lip; maker's mark).

The bulbous body of the cann is engraved with the coat of arms of the Hodges family, and the bottom is engraved with Joseph Hodges's initials:
H
I E
Joseph Hodges is probably Captain Joseph Hodges of Salem, Massachusetts, a Revolutionary War patriot.

32

George II covered tankard

LONDON, ENGLAND, 1758–59
PRODUCED BY THOMAS WHIPHAM (D. 1815)
AND CHARLES WRIGHT
H 10 in. (25.4 cm), D 5⁷⁄₁₆ in. (13.8 cm)
BEQUEST OF B. PAGE MARSDEN 51.1.1

Hallmarks (struck on inside cover and on bottom): C/TW/W (maker's mark); Leopard head crowned (London assay); Lion passant (sterling standard); Black letter capital C (date letter for 1758–59).

This large, baluster-shaped covered tankard is raised on a stepped foot ring. The two sections of the body are joined by a molded band. It has an applied scroll handle, cast and hollow, with a vent at the base. The body is engraved with the script initials JMM. The stepped domed lid has an applied shell thumbpiece.

33

Covered tankard

BOSTON, MASSACHUSETTS, C. 1769
PRODUCED BY BENJAMIN BURT (1729–1805)
H 9 in. (22.9 cm), D 5⅜ in. (13.7 cm)
71.804

Hallmarks (stamped to left of handle near lip): BENJAMIN/BURT (maker's mark).

Benjamin Burt, a contemporary of Paul Revere and one of the most patronized silversmiths of his day, probably made this tankard at the order of William Hyslop (1713–96) for his son, David, and his wife. The couple handed it down engraved on the handle with their initials:

H
D E
The bottom script engraving J H to/ Mary C Shannon/1849 was added in 1849. J H was probably a member of the Hyslop family. Around 1849, due to a wave of temperance reform, a spout was attached to the front of this tankard below the middle. It is fortunate that no other alteration was made, since many tankards were ruined by the addition of lips. The spout has since been removed and the opening closed with a soldered-in circlet of silver.

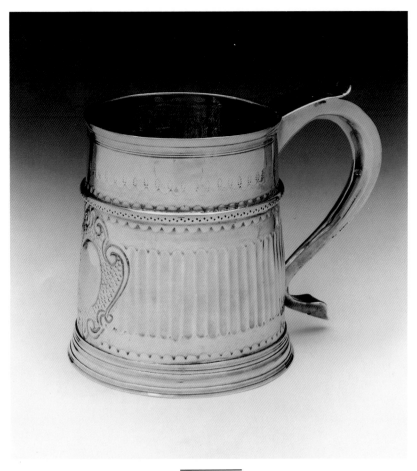

28

29

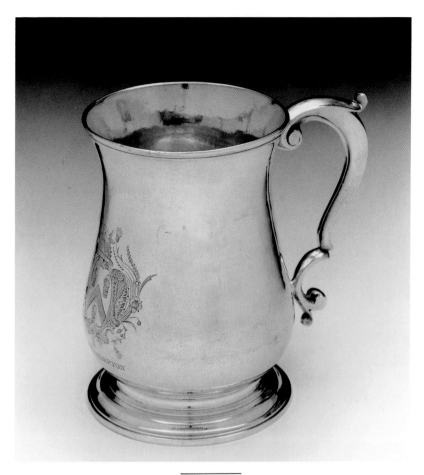

30

31

32

33

34

James I beaker

LONDON, ENGLAND, C. 1618–19
PRODUCED BY UNIDENTIFIED MAKER
H 6⅜ in. (16.2 cm), D 3¾ in. (9.5 cm)
78.76

Hallmarks (struck on bottom): Eagle displayed (unidentified maker's mark); Lion passant (sterling standard); Crowned leopard head (London assay); Italic small a (date letter for 1618–19).

This trumpet-shaped beaker has interlaced strapwork and scrolling foliage with clusters of leaves and flowers.

35

Covered parcel-gilt beaker

RIGA, RUSSIA, C. 1740
PRODUCED BY JOHANN DIETRICH REHWALD
(REVALD)
H 11¾ in. (29.8 cm), D 5⅞ in. (14.9 cm)
GIFT OF ROBERT A. MILLS 77.1231.24a–b

Hallmarks (struck on lip of cover and bottom of beaker): Crossed keys (mark of the city of Riga); IDR (maker's mark); D (unknown mark); Engraved Cyrillic E (beaker); Engraved Cyrillic III (Ripida).

This beaker comes from the Romanoff collection and was sold in New York in February 1931, catalogue no. 289, Wallace H. Day Galleries. It bears an engraved coat of arms, which is unidentified, and another engraving around the lip dated 1762, which memorializes a man named Carl Jacob Dorre.

36

Parcel-gilt cup

MOSCOW, RUSSIA, 1747
PRODUCED BY UNIDENTIFIED MAKER
H 9¹³⁄₁₆ in. (24.9 cm), D 3⅝ in. (9.2 cm)
GIFT OF ROBERT A. MILLS 77.1231.23

Hallmarks (struck on foot and just under lip of cup): AS (Andrey Zaytsev—Moscow assayer, 1735–49); St. George killing the dragon/1747 (Moscow city mark).

This cup comes from the Romanoff collection and was sold in New York in February 1931, catalogue no. 286, Wallace H. Day Galleries. It is especially interesting for its filigree cage set with oval chased parcel-gilt portraits of Peter the Great, Catherine, and Elizabeth. The foot and stem are chased and engraved with stylized leafage.

37

Art deco cocktail goblet

NEWBURYPORT, MASSACHUSETTS, C. 1930
PRODUCED BY OLD NEWBURY CRAFTERS, INC.
H 7 in. (17.8 cm), D 2½ in. (6.4 cm)
80.199

Hallmarks (struck on bottom): Eagle displayed (manufacturer's mark); Sterling (silver standard); 104 (design number ?).

The cast round foot of this tall goblet is slightly domed and fits into a black enamel stem that tapers slightly until it joins the bowl. The cast bowl is decorated with a stylized arch design of black and red enamel.

38

Art deco cocktail shaker

ATTLEBORO, MASSACHUSETTS, C. 1930
PRODUCED BY WATSON COMPANY
H 10¾ in. (27.3 cm), D 3½ in. (8.9 cm)
80.196

Hallmarks (struck on bottom): Crown, W, Lion passant (trade mark); Sterling silver (silver standard); B359 (design number ?).

This plain shaker has a sectioned body and an applied handle, perhaps of Bakelite. The top is made in two sections, a cap and a strainer.

39

Charles II two-handled covered caudle cup

LONDON, ENGLAND, C. 1672–73
PRODUCED BY UNIDENTIFIED MAKER
H 7½ in. (19.1 cm), D 6 in. (15.2 cm)
78.77

Hallmarks (struck below lip; maker's mark struck only on cover): TK (maker's mark); Leopard head crowned (London assay); Lion passant (sterling standard); Black letter capital P (date letter for 1672–73).

The bulbous body is of light-gauge silver. On it appear chased designs of large flowers and leaves with chased engraved cartouches bearing a different set of unidentified arms on each side. The applied scroll handles are cast in the form of caryatids. The domed cover is similarly decorated and has a double-knob finial. It was designed to contain caudle or posset, which was hot milk curdled with ale or wine and seasoned with spices.

34

35

36

37

38

39

Ceremonial Vessels

40

George I two-handled cup

DUBLIN, IRELAND, 1723–24
PRODUCED BY WILLIAM DUGGAN
H 6¾ in. (17.2 cm), D 5½ in. (14.0 cm)
78.84

Hallmarks (struck on bottom): Crowned harp (duty mark); Old English capital D (date letter for 1723–24); WD (maker's mark). Other marks (engraved on bottom): F (unidentified).

The gently flaring body of this cup is plain with no engraving. It has an applied stepped foot ring and an applied lip and midband. Two cast double-scroll handles are attached.

41

George II two-handled covered cup

LONDON, ENGLAND, 1733-34
PRODUCED BY DAVID WILLIAUME II (1693–1761)
H 12 in. (30.5 cm), D 6½ in. (16.5 cm)
78.121

Hallmarks (struck on bottom and lip of cover—cover does not have maker's mark): DW (maker's mark); Leopard head crowned (London assay); Lion passant (sterling standard); Roman capital S (date letter for 1733–34).

The cup is raised on a broad domed foot decorated with strapwork, formed of pierced strips of silver with chased and scrolled moldings, applied to a matte background. The two scroll handles are applied. The domed cover has a cast, chased, applied finial in a flattened acorn shape. Surprisingly little of David Williaume's Huguenot background is reflected by the silver that bears his mark; it is thought that much of this work was accomplished by English journeymen in his employ.

42

George III two-handled covered cup

LONDON, ENGLAND, 1780–81
PRODUCED BY ROBERT HENNELL I (1741–1811)
H 15 in. (38.1 cm), D 6¼ in. (15.9 cm)
78.103

Hallmarks (struck on foot of cup and lip of cover): R H (maker's mark); Lion passant (sterling standard); Leopard head crowned (London assay); Roman small e (date letter for 1780–81).

Neoclassical in design, this covered cup is raised above a high foot decorated with a band of beading and a chased band of scrolls and tulips against a stippled ground. The main body of the cup is decorated with a band of chased leaves and with chased swags and ribbons looped over an oval patera. An unidentified coat of arms is engraved under the lip on one side with the motto Fide Et Virtute (Fidelity and Virtue). The spool-shaped cover is decorated with bands of beading at the lip and below the finial, which is urn-shaped and set on chased leaves. The cover has a band of scrolling that matches the base, and an unidentified crest is engraved on it. The cup has two hollow cast handles decorated with beading on each side and joined to the body with leaflike decorations.

There were five generations of Hennell silversmiths in London, beginning with David I (1712–85) and ending with James (1829–99). The family business ceased with the death of James.

43

Commemorative covered urn

NORFOLK, VIRGINIA, 1821
PRODUCED BY JOHN POTTER
H 17½ in. (44.5 cm), D 10 in. (25.4 cm)
RECEIVED FROM THE INDEPENDENCE NATIONAL HISTORICAL PARK PROJECT 54.57.1

Hallmarks (struck twice on foot and once on bottom): J. POTTER (maker's mark); NORFOLK (city of manufacture).

John Potter went to Norfolk from Alexandria in 1816 and took Henry H. Redman as his partner in 1819. This firm lasted until July 1821, when Potter again worked on his own. It was at this time that the citizens of Norfolk commissioned him to create this covered urn-shaped vessel, which is decorated with applied stamped bands of flowers and leaves and is mounted on each side with lion-mask handles. The cover is surmounted by a pineapple and leaves. The urn was presented to attorney Caesar A. Rodney for his successful defense of Commodore James Barron of Norfolk, who was charged with negligence in surrendering his ship to a British frigate in 1807. The gift was inscribed in Latin with the words "To Caesar A. Rodney, jurist outstanding as much in capacity as in knowledge, who, when he had seen his fellow citizen, James Barron, distinguished commander in the American navy, threatened with a cruel fate, could not endure the sight of an occurrence so unworthy, but to the glory of his name, rushed to his aid, protected him, and wrested him from danger. This token of regard the citizenry of Norfolk gives and dedicates with a grateful heart."

40

41

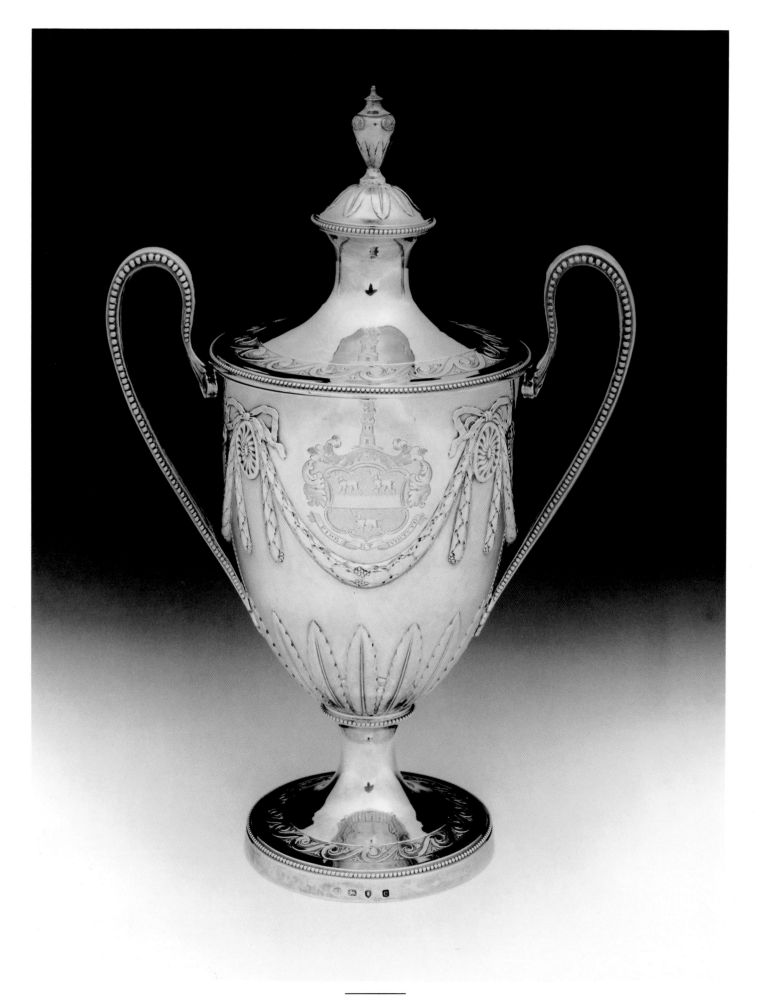

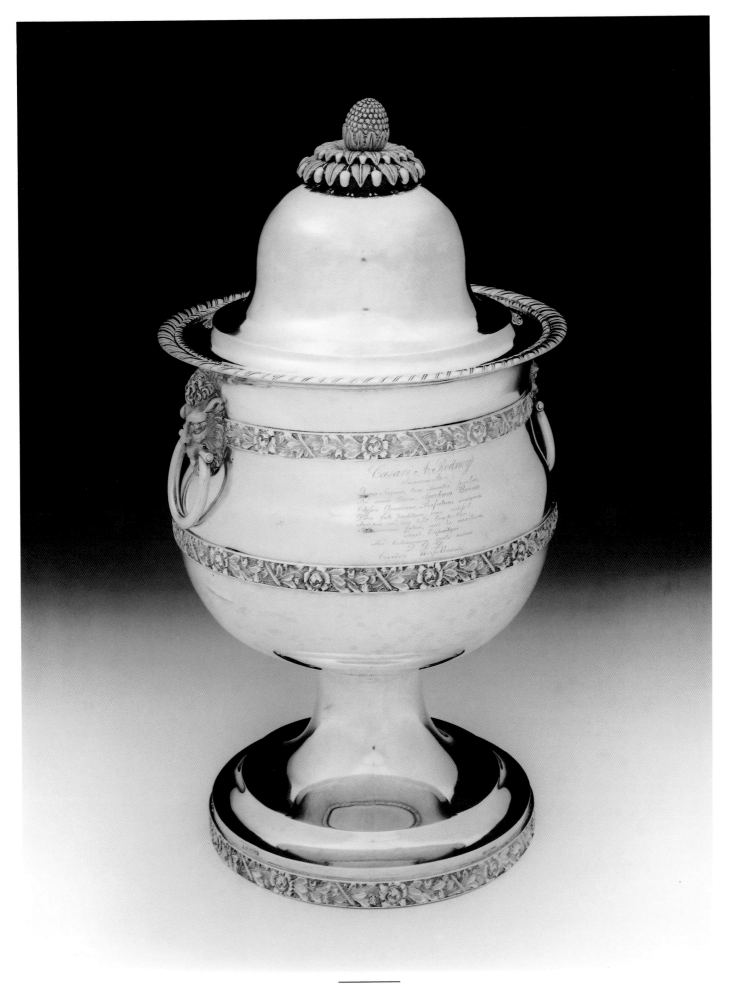

44

George III covered presentaton cup

LONDON, ENGLAND, 1817–18
PRODUCED BY PAUL STORR (1771–1844)
H 13 in. (33.0 cm), D 8¾ in. (22.2 cm)
GIFT IN HONOR OF ROY B. MARTIN, JR. 78.88

Hallmarks (full marks struck on side of cup near handle; partial marks on inside of cover and partial marks on bottom of finial): PS (maker's mark); Lion passant (sterling standard); Leopard head crowned (London assay); Roman small b (date letter for 1817–18); King's head (duty stamp). Other marks (inscribed around foot): RUNDELL BRIDGE ET RUNDELL AURIFICES REGIS ET PRINCIPIS WALLIAE REGENTIS BRITANNIAS FECERUNT LONDINI [Made in London by Rundell Bridge and Rundell, Goldsmiths to the King and to the Prince of Wales, Regent of Britain].

The foot, cast and plain except for a band of stylized leafage and flower heads, is applied to the fluted bottom of the campana-shaped cup. The cup is formed in two parts, with an applied band of figures that are part man, part horse, and part fish holding a trident aloft. There is a seashell between these figures on the front and back. Above this is an applied wreath of leaves and fruit, and within one wreath is engraved Charleston Races/South Carolina/February 1818. There are two applied cast handles formed of twisted grapevines ending in leaves and fruit and attached under the rim. The bottoms of the handles are attached where the foot joins the cup. The domed cover is engraved with four sections of stars and stripes separated by leafy vines and engraved with the directional signs E S W and a fleur-de-lys. The finial is in the form of an eagle clutching an olive branch and lightning bolts. The entire cup and cover are silver gilt and probably stood on a square base that is now missing.

Paul Storr was one of the most popular silversmiths of the Regency period. His mark is on many of the monumental and majestic objects in silver and silver gilt. It is not certain just how much work bearing Storr's mark was actually made or designed by him, since he had a huge workshop with designers and journeymen. In general Storr seems not to have been very inventive. He often copied the designs of his teacher, Andrew Fogelburg, and repeatedly reused castings made in the workshops under him. Having worked on his own and in partnership with William Frisbee for a short time, Storr worked exclusively for the Royal goldsmiths, Rundell, Bridge and Rundell, from 1807 until 1819.

45

Martelé loving cup/wine cooler

PROVIDENCE, RHODE ISLAND, 1900
PRODUCED BY THE GORHAM MANUFACTURING COMPANY
H 9¼ in. (23.5 cm), D 8¼ in. (21.0 cm)
71.980

Hallmarks (stamped on bottom): Martelé (name of the line); Lion (silver); Eagle over an anchor (symbol of Rhode Island); G (for Gorham); 950-1000 fine (grade of silver); CMF (date mark for 1900).

The cup has a waisted raised body with a ruffled flaring mouth. The body is chased with designs in the art nouveau style with water lilies, buds, leaves, and stems, the stems forming reserves. Three feet are drawn out of the body and sit under the applied chased handles, which are hollow, cast, and chased in the same design as the body.

Art deco covered cup or vase

PARIS, FRANCE, C. 1930
PRODUCED BY G. KELLER
H 13¾ in. (34.9 cm), D 6¾ in. (17.2 cm)
87.54

Hallmarks: Struck on lip of cover: Head of Minerva (mark for grade of silver); G. Keller (maker's name); G K in a lozenge (maker's mark). Struck on side of cup near lip: Head of Minerva (mark for grade of silver). Struck on bottom: G. Keller (maker's name); Paris (city of production); GK in a square (maker's mark ?). Struck on side of base: G. Keller (maker's name); GK in a lozenge (maker's mark).

This cup or vase has a paneled trumpet-shaped body, twin angular lapis lazuli handles applied near the rim, and a ribbed domed base raised over an octagonal platform inset with lapis lazuli panels. The fitted ribbed cover has a lapis lazuli finial. This is an elegant example of art deco work by a silversmith named G. Keller, about whom no information is available. It is possible that he was a German working in Paris who marked this piece with the official French mark of a lozenge and placed his German mark GK in a square.

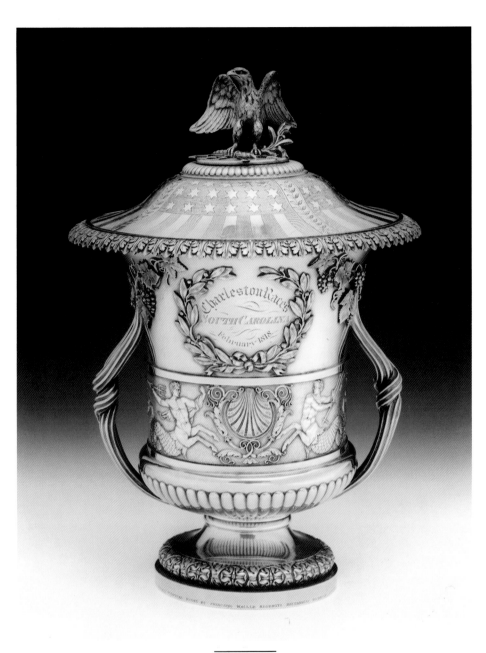

44

46

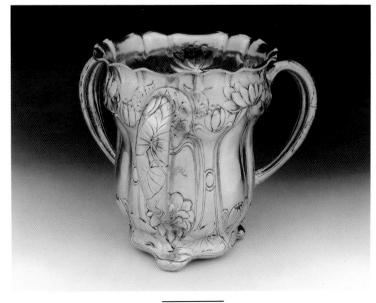

45

Service of Wine and Water

47

Martelé punch bowl

PROVIDENCE, RHODE ISLAND, 1900
PRODUCED BY THE GORHAM MANUFACTURING
COMPANY
H 14 in. (35.6 cm), D 13¼ in. (33.7 cm)
83.528

Hallmarks (struck on bottom): Lion (silver); Eagle over an anchor (symbol of Rhode Island); G (for Gorham); 950-1000 fine, encircled (quality of silver with the encircling indicating a custom order); 2518 (mark for year 1900).

This extremely large and heavy punch bowl is decorated with art nouveau designs of chased flowers and leaves, with female figures chased under and around the ruffled lip. Two hollow handles are applied and chased with female figures, full length and nude, among flowers and foliage. The constricted foot is ruffled and chased with leafage, and the interior has been gilded. The bottom is engraved with a monogram and the date 1900.

48

Martelé punch ladle

PROVIDENCE, RHODE ISLAND, 1905
PRODUCED BY THE GORHAM MANUFACTURING
COMPANY
L 13½ in. (34.3 cm)
71.975

Hallmarks (struck on bottom of bowl): Lion (silver); Eagle over an anchor (symbol of Rhode Island); G (for Gorham); 9584/JGG (marks for year 1905).

This punch ladle is hammered from a heavy piece of silver and chased with designs of flowers and leaves in a manner typical of the art nouveau style. The conjoined monogram MEW is chased on the interior of the bowl. This ladle was not made to go with the preceding punch bowl (no. 47).

49

Claret jug

FRANKFURT, GERMANY, C. 1890
PRODUCED BY G.F. KEYSER
H 11¼ in. (28.6 cm), D 5 in. (12.7 cm)
77.617

Hallmarks (struck on bottom and on shoulder left of handle): G.F. Keyser (maker's mark); Moon and crown (German silver standard); Eagle (mark of Frankfurt); An illegible mark.

The cut-glass body is fitted into a stamped base that is decorated with a band of leafage and beading. The glass is surmounted by a neck and pouring spout stamped and decorated with stylized leafage and an applied wreath with griffins on each side. The cover is gilded on the interior and has a thumbpiece formed of leafage. The applied handle is scrolled, cast, and hollow and has cast and applied designs of leafage, flower heads, and grapes.

This jug was used for serving claret (Bordeaux red wine), and probably for other liquids as well. Earlier examples are made entirely of silver, but most of the jugs seen now are of cut or frosted glass.

50

Water pitcher

BALTIMORE, MARYLAND, 1846–61
PRODUCED BY SAMUEL KIRK AND SON
H 14¼ in. (36.2 cm), D 5¾ in. (14.6 cm)
77.541

Hallmarks (struck on bottom): S. KIRK & SON (manufacturing company); 11.OZ (liquid capacity of pitcher).

This baluster-shaped pitcher has a hollow, cast, applied handle decorated with a ram's head, flowers, and foliage. Most of the pitcher is covered with repoussé and chased designs of flowers, foliage, and buildings, including images of a figure washing in a fountain and gardens with potted flowers. The background is mostly stippled.

Kirk (now Kirk Stieff Co.) is the oldest continuously working silversmith firm in this country. The company became famous for its repoussé pattern, which it began using before 1822 and which was probably influenced by similar work done by the Dutch.

51

Water pitcher

PHILADELPHIA, PENNSYLVANIA, C.1900
PRODUCED BY BAILEY, BANKS, AND BIDDLE
COMPANY
H 12 in. (30.5 cm), D 7 in. (17.8 cm)
77.571

Hallmarks (struck on bottom): THE BAILEY BANKS & BIDDLE/925/1000/COMPANY (maker and grade of silver); BBB (maker's mark); 925 (grade of silver); S (unknown); 1210 (pattern number); 6P'T'S (measure); Sterling (silver standard).

This baluster-shaped jug is raised from a round stepped foot and decorated with art nouveau designs of water lilies, leaves, and other water flowers chased up the lobed sides of the jug in high relief. The applied handle is decorated with chased and applied cattails spreading around the lip of the pitcher.

47

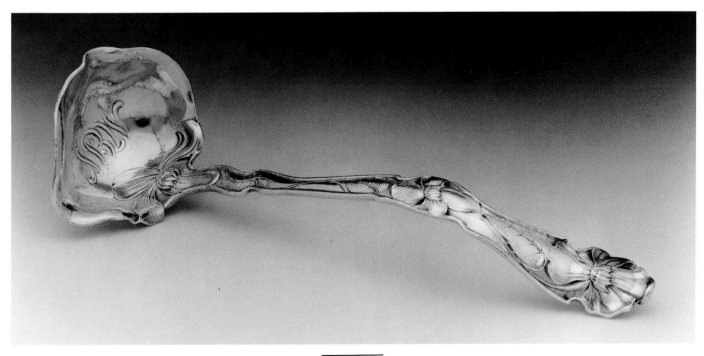

48

50

51

Tea and Coffee: From Exotic to Everyday

T ea and coffee were first enjoyed by Europeans in the seventeenth century as expensive and exotic luxuries. Ceramists and silversmiths recognized that the growing taste for the beverages brought with it a need for wares to prepare and serve coffee and tea. Potters led the way in the production of vessels for these drinks, many of their designs inspired by wares imported from the East. By the end of the seventeenth century, however, silver teapots and coffeepots began to appear on the tables of the wealthy and sophisticated. Because of the expense of the beverages and their limited availability, early teapots tended to be rather small, growing in size during the eighteenth century as the drink became an everyday ritual. The number of objects required for the tea service multiplied as well—caddies for the dried leaves, waste bowls, sugar bowls, cream or milk jugs, hot-water kettles, and spoons. Sets of silver tea utensils might at first have consisted of pieces dated and decorated slightly differently, but by the late eighteenth century matched services were the order of the day.

In the nineteenth century afternoon entertainment at home became quite common, especially among middle-class women. Most of these events centered around the tea table, and considerable effort and expense were directed toward the acquisition of an extensive matched tea service, which might include more than one teapot (for different varieties of tea), a hot-water kettle on a stand, and vessels for sugar and milk. The spread of tea drinking stimulated production in both ceramics and silver. Large firms capitalized on the growing market by offering their manufactured silver for sale through retail outlets or printed catalogues.

In the United States the growth of the silver industry was closely linked to the emergence of a large middle class. Small silversmithing workshops, family run and with limited staff, were overshadowed by large, efficiently organized, and industrially oriented firms, many of which produced silver tea services alongside a line of less expensive silver-plated wares. By the early decades of this century the silver tea service was becoming a luxury as silver prices rose steeply and elaborate afternoon teas declined in popularity. With a more informal style pervading middle-class households, and with women participating more fully in a range of activities that went well beyond their traditionally assigned role in the home, the silver tea service became a quaint reminder of days gone by, relegated to formal use on special occasions. Silversmiths continued to produce tea services, as the twentieth-century sets in the Chrysler collection attest, but most of these sets no doubt served primarily as display items.

52

George I teapot

DUBLIN, IRELAND, 1718–19
PRODUCED BY UNIDENTIFIED MAKER
H 5 in. (11.4 cm), L 9 in. (22.9 cm),
W 4½ in. (10.8 cm)
78.82

Hallmarks (struck on bottom): Crowned harp (mark for Dublin and sovereign's mark); Court-hand B (date letter for 1718–19); Maker's mark obliterated. Other marks (crudely cut into bottom): IG/15 '14 (perhaps an inventory number).

This pot has a globular body, a short round applied foot ring, and a flat cover with a slightly raised ring and a heavy applied hinge in a double T shape. The turned wood finial on the cover is raised on a silver ring with a ball top. The spout is plain and applied, and the scroll handle fits into two tapered silver sockets applied to the body.

53

Louis XVI coffeepot

PARIS, FRANCE, C. 1783–89
PRODUCED BY NICOLAS-CHRYSOSTOME CAUET
H 7 in. (17.8 cm)
77.595

Hallmarks (struck on bottom): A, formed of a crown, trumpet, and leafage (Paris charge mark); Crown, fleur-de-lys, bird, and NC (maker's mark); Obliterated mark. Other marks (stamped on rims of both pot and cover): Bird head and obliterated mark (discharge marks).

This is a pear-shaped coffeepot with attached cover, thumbpiece, and cast finial. A transverse handle of ebony fits into an applied silver socket and an applied pouring spout. Three splayed feet are applied to the body. The pot is decorated with swags of flowers, leafage, and ribbons tied into finely chased and repoussé bows.

54

Coffeepot

NEW YORK, NEW YORK, C. 1800
PRODUCED BY HUGH WISHART
(ACTIVE 1793–1837)
H 15 in. (38.1 cm), L 14 in. (35.6 cm),
W 5½ in. (14.0 cm)
80.227

Hallmarks (struck on foot): WISHART, in a rectangle (maker's mark).

This tall urn-shaped covered pot has an applied spout and a wooden scroll handle fitted into two silver sockets and applied to the body. There is a thumb rest near the top of the handle. The pot is plain except for engraved bands of bright-cut leaves and swags around the top of the body. It also displays wavy and dotted lines and, on the cover, a band of chevronlike designs. Each side has a cartouche that is bright cut in the design of a shield, surrounded by drapery, cords, and tassels and engraved with the initials DH in script. This coffeepot is a handsome example of the federal style, which appeared in the United States in the transition between rococo and classical revival styles.

55

George III four-piece tea and coffee service

LONDON, ENGLAND, 1810–11
PRODUCED BY SAMUEL HENNELL (B. 1778)
78.71a–d

Teapot

H 6¼ in. (15.9 cm), L 11¼ in. (28.6 cm),
W 5 in. (12.7 cm)
78.71a

Hallmarks (struck on bottom): SH (maker's mark); Crowned leopard head (London assay); Lion passant (sterling standard); Roman capital P (date letter for 1810–11); King's head (duty stamp).

This rectangular teapot has a bold fluted body, an applied spout, and a hollow cast scroll handle with two ivory insulators and an applied shell thumbpiece. The top of the pot has a band of gadrooning, with shells and leaves applied at each of the four corners. The hinged cover is fluted and surmounted by a fluted finial. The pot stands on four ball feet.

Cream jug

H 3⅞ in. (9.9 cm), L 6 in. (15.2 cm),
W 3⅜ in. (8.6 cm)
78.71b

Hallmarks (struck in open area under spout): Marked the same as the teapot (78.71a) except the maker's mark is rubbed out.

This rectangular cream jug has a bold fluted body, an applied scroll handle with an applied shell thumbpiece, a gadrooned rim, and two shells and leaves applied at the handle end. Its interior is gilded, and it is raised on four ball feet.

Coffeepot

H 8¾ in. (22.2 cm), L 11¼ in. (28.6 cm),
W 5¾ in. (14.6 cm)
78.71c

Hallmarks (struck on right edge of base): Marked the same as the teapot (78.71a).

The bold fluted body of this rectangular coffeepot has an applied hollow scroll handle with two ivory insulators, and an applied spout. The handle has a shell applied as a thumbpiece. The pot is raised on a rectangular pedestal base with four ball feet, and its top edge has a band of applied gadrooning with a shell and leaf applied at each corner. The hinged cover is fluted and surmounted by a fluted finial.

Sugar bowl

H 4 in. (10.2 cm), L 8¼ in. (21.0 cm),
W 4⅜ in. (11.1 cm)
78.71d

Hallmarks (struck on side above fluting): Marked the same as the teapot (78.71a).

This rectangular open sugar bowl has a bold fluted body, an applied hollow scroll handle with a shell thumbpiece, and an applied gadroon border at its lip with applied shell and leaf at each corner. It is raised on four ball feet.

52

53

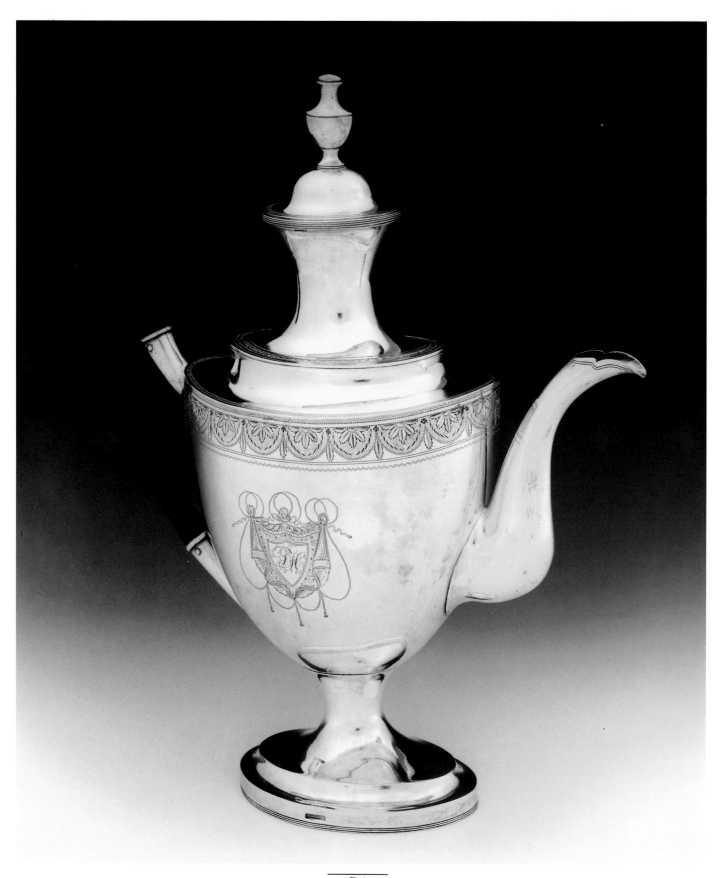

54

55

56

Teapot

PHILADELPHIA, PENNSYLVANIA, C. 1815–22
PRODUCED BY FLETCHER AND GARDINER
(THOMAS FLETCHER AND SIDNEY GARDINER)
H 9¾ in. (24.8 cm), L 11¼ in. (28.6 cm),
D 6¼ in. (15.9 cm)
77.540

Hallmarks (struck on bottom): FLETCHER & GARDINER in a circle with PHILA in the center of the circle (manufacturing company and city of production).

A band of applied shell and leafage decorates this inverted pear-shaped teapot at its broadest point. The applied spout has a large leaf applied to its underside and another at its end. There is a band of flowers and leaves where the base is applied to the body, and the base is stepped and decorated with a bead variant, as is the mouth of the main body. The hinged lid is chased and repoussé with a design of leaves and is surmounted by a basket-shaped finial. The light wood handle, scroll-shaped and carved with a thumbpiece, is joined to the body with leaf-shaped sockets.

57

Three-piece tea service

BOSTON, MASSACHUSETTS, C. 1840
PRODUCED BY OBIDIAH RICH (ACTIVE C. 1832–50)
BEQUEST OF MISS FLORENCE L. SMITH
52.18.212a–c

Teapot
H 7 in. (17.8 cm), L 10½ in. (26.7 cm),
D 6¼ in. (15.9 cm)
52.18.212a

Hallmarks (struck on bottom): O. Rich. (producer); fine (grade of silver?); BOSTON (city of production).

This globular paneled teapot has an applied hollow scroll handle with two ivory insulators and an applied curved spout. The handle fits onto the pot and bears applied leaf-shaped decorations. The four claw feet are surmounted by leaves and applied to the body. The cover is surmounted by a swan.

Covered sugar bowl
H 6¼ in. (15.9 cm), L 8¼ in. (21.0 cm),
D 5½ in. (14.0 cm)
52.18.212b

Hallmarks (struck on bottom): Marked the same as the teapot (58.18.212a).

This globular paneled sugar bowl has hollow applied scroll-shaped handles with leaf decorations applied to each. Four leaf-and-paw feet are applied to the body. The cover, surmounted by a swan, is not hinged.

Cream jug
H 6¼ in. (15.9 cm), L 5¼ in. (13.3 cm),
D 3¾ in. (9.5 cm)
52.18.212c

Hallmarks (struck on bottom): Marked the same as the teapot (58.18.212a).

The bulbous paneled body of this jug has an applied scroll-shaped hollow handle and four paw feet surmounted by leaf-shaped decorations. The body is drawn up to form the lip.

58

Three-piece tea service

NEW YORK, NEW YORK, C. 1856
PRODUCED BY BALL, BLACK AND COMPANY
(1851–76)
77.536a–c

Covered sugar bowl
H 7¼ in. (18.4 cm), D 5¾ in. (14.6 cm)
77.536a

Hallmarks (struck on bottom): BALL. BLACK&CO (maker); NEW YORK (city of manufacture).

The bulbous covered sugar bowl has two angular applied strap handles. Each is decorated with beading and a female head and terminates in a palm leaf where the handles join the lower body of the bowl. The cover flares out to fit the rim of the body and rises to a narrow neck supporting an applied cast finial in the form of a Greek or Roman military helmet resting on a beaded round base. The bowl has a stepped foot ring, and the initial C is engraved on the side.

Hot-milk jug
H 7½ in. (19.1 cm), D 4½ in. (11.4 cm)
77.536b

Hallmarks (struck on bottom): 925/1000 (silver standard); 1856 (engraved date).

This bulbous covered milk jug has a slender neck, an applied spout, and a cover with a cast applied finial in the form of a Greek or Roman military helmet resting on a round beaded base. The jug has an applied strap handle and two insulators. The handle is decorated with beading and a female head and terminates in a palm leaf where it joins the lower body. The pot is raised on a stepped foot ring, and the initial C is engraved on the side.

Teapot
H 9⅜ in. (23.8 cm), D 6 in. (15.2 cm)
77.536c

Hallmarks (struck on bottom): Marked the same as the sugar bowl (77.536a); 1856 (engraved date).

This bulbous teapot has a slender neck, a tall applied spout, and a hollow handle decorated with beading and a female head. The handle terminates in a palm leaf where it joins the body and has two ivory insulators. Its cover has an applied finial in the form of a Greek or Roman military helmet. The pot is raised on a stepped foot ring, and the initial C is engraved on the side.

56

57

58

59

Coffeepot

NEW YORK, NEW YORK, C. 1856–59
PRODUCED BY TIFFANY AND COMPANY
H 9¼ in. (23.5 cm), L 9¼ in. (23.5 cm),
W 4½ in. (11.4 cm)
77.534a

Hallmarks: Old English capital M (Edward C. Moore, head of silver works; struck on left foot); 844 5997 (pattern and order number; struck on right foot); TIFFANY & CO./STERLING (maker and silver standard; struck on rear foot).

This coffeepot takes its design from earlier Empire prototypes. The egg-shaped body is raised on a tripod of elongated legs applied to the body of the pot and has female heads with birds on each side. The feet terminate in hairy paws. Bands of rolled borders are applied below the lip, at the rim, and on the edge of the slightly domed top. The border is of a leaf design. The spout has a hinged cover, and the transverse wooden handle is baluster-shaped and applied at the neck.

60

Martelé black coffeepot

PROVIDENCE, RHODE ISLAND, 1905
PRODUCED BY GORHAM MANUFACTURING COMPANY
H 12 in. (30.5 cm), L 6¾ in. (17.2 cm),
D 5 in. (12.7 cm)
83.523

Hallmarks (struck on bottom): Martelé (name of the line); Lion (silver); Eagle over an anchor (symbol for Rhode Island); G (for Gorham); .9584 HGJ (indicates date of 1905).

This black coffeepot is chased with an art nouveau design of flowers and leaves with elongated stems. A long curving spout is applied to the body, as is an elongated scroll handle with two ivory insulators. The pot's shape bespeaks a slight Turkish influence. The base, lip, and cover are ruffled, and the cover bears a finial resembling a water lily. The initials GL are engraved on the right side.

61

Six-piece tea and coffee service

COPENHAGEN, DENMARK, C. 1933-45
PRODUCED BY GEORG JENSEN (1866-1935)
87.57.1–6

Tray

H 1¾ in. (4.5 cm), L 24½ in. (62.2 cm),
W 14½ in. (36.8 cm)
87.57.1

Hallmarks (struck on bottom near one handle): 925.S (sterling standard); DENMARK (country of origin); JG (maker's mark used 1933–45); STERLING (silver standard); 2 K (perhaps the number in a service).

The end of each handle on this plain oval tray is formed of Blossom-pattern flowers and leaves.

Coffeepot

H 8 in. (20.3 cm), W 8¼ in. (21.0 cm)
87.57.2a–b

Hallmarks (struck on bottom): 925.S (silver standard); Denmark (country of origin); GEORG JENSEN in a dotted oval (maker's mark used 1945 to present); Sterling (silver standard); 2 C (perhaps the number in a service).

This coffeepot is of ovoid shape with an ivory transverse handle and an applied spout. It is raised on three applied zoomorphic feet and surmounted by a loose cover chased in the form of leaves with a Blossom-pattern finial. This design, first produced in 1904, is still in production.

Teapot

H 5 in. (12.7 cm), W 8½ in. (21.6 cm)
87.57.3a–b

Hallmarks (struck on bottom): GEORG JENSEN in a dotted oval (maker's mark used 1945 to present); 925.S (silver standard); Sterling Denmark (silver standard and country of origin); 2 B (perhaps the number in a service).

This squat round teapot has an applied transverse handle of ivory and an applied spout. It is raised on three applied zoomorphic feet and is surmounted with a loose cover, which is chased in the form of leaves and has a cast Blossom-pattern finial.

Cream jug

H 2¼ in. (5.7 cm), L 5 in. (12.7 cm)
87.57.4

Hallmarks (struck on bottom): 925.S (silver standard); Sterling and GEORG JENSEN in dotted oval (silver standard and maker's mark used 1945 to present); 2 B (perhaps the number in a service).

This squat round cream jug has an applied ivory transverse handle and is raised on three applied zoomorphic feet.

Covered sugar bowl

H 3½ in. (8.9 cm), D 3⁵⁄₁₆ in. (8.4 cm)
87.57.5a–b

Hallmarks (struck on bottom); GEORG JENSEN in dotted oval (maker's mark used 1945 to present); 925.S (silver standard); Denmark sterling (country of origin and silver standard); 2 C (perhaps the number in a service).

The tapered body of this squat round sugar bowl is raised on three applied zoomorphic feet and is covered with a domed lid chased with a leaf design and a cast applied Blossom-pattern finial.

Tea strainer on stand

H 1¾ in. (4.5 cm), L 4⅞ in. (12.4 cm),
D 2⅞ in. (7.3 cm)
87.57.6a–b

Hallmarks: Strainer (87.57.6a, struck on bottom): GEORG JENSEN in a dotted oval (maker's mark used 1945 to present); Sterling (silver standard); Denmark (country of origin); 84 (unknown); B (unknown). Stand (87.57.6b, struck on bottom): 925.S (silver standard); Denmark (country of origin); GEORG JENSEN in a dotted oval (maker's mark used 1945 to present); Sterling (silver standard); 77B (unknown).

This strainer is round and pierced, with an applied fan-shaped ivory handle that has applied Blossom-pattern flowers. The strainer rests on a round drip cup with three applied zoomorphic feet.

59

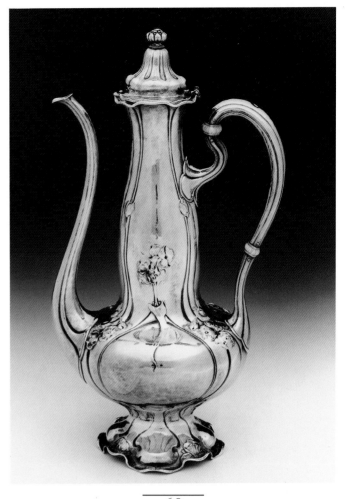

60

61

62

Art deco four-piece tea and coffee service

PARIS, FRANCE, 1935
DESIGNED BY JEAN PUIFORCAT
PRODUCED BY MAISON PUIFORCAT
87.72.1–4

Coffeepot
H 5½ in. (14.0 cm), L 7½ in. (19.1 cm),
D 5 in. (12.7 cm)
87.72.1a–b

Hallmarks (struck on bottom of pot and handle and on inside of cover): EP within a lozenge (maker's mark); JEAN E. PUIFORCAT (maker's name; bottom of pot only); Head of Minerva (silver standard).

This tapering round coffeepot has a threaded lip and an angular applied spout and handle. The handle and cover are of Brazilian rosewood, and the cover is inlaid with the silver initials DP conjoined. The pattern of this service is named Tulip.

Teapot
H 3¼ in. (8.3 cm), L 8¼ in. (21.0 cm),
D 5¼ in. (13.3 cm)
87.72.2a–b

Hallmarks: Marked the same as the coffeepot (87.72.1a–b).

Sugar bowl
H 3⅛ in. (7.9 cm), L 5⁵⁄₁₆ in. (13.5 cm),
D 4⅛ in. (10.5 cm)
87.72.3a–b

Hallmarks: Marked the same as the coffeepot (87.72.1a–b).

In place of the spout found on the pots (87.72.1a–b and 87.72.2a–b) there is a second handle. Both handles are silver and the cover is rosewood.

Cream jug
H 3 in. (7.6 cm), L 4½ in. (11.4 cm),
D 2¹¹⁄₁₆ in. (6.8 cm)
87.72.4a–b

Hallmarks: Marked the same as the coffeepot (87.72.1a–b).

63

Cream jug

BOSTON, MASSACHUSETTS, C. 1765
PRODUCED BY BENJAMIN BURT (1729–1805)
H 3½ in. (8.9 cm), L 4 in. (10.2 cm),
D 1¾ in. (4.5 cm)
71.821

Hallmarks (struck on bottom): B.BURT (maker's mark). Other marks: Engraved initials MPE between front legs.

The bulbous round body of this jug is rather straight below the flaring scalloped rim with its applied lip extension. A cast double-scroll handle with a modeled grip is affixed with a triangle over the rim. It has three cast cabriole legs with modeled pad joinings and slightly angled trifid feet.

64

George III cream jug

LONDON, ENGLAND, 1765–66
PRODUCED BY SAMUEL MERITON I
H 4⅛ in. (10.5 cm), L 4¼ in. (10.8 cm),
D 2¾ in. (7.0 cm)
78.66

Hallmarks (struck on right side of handle just below rim): SM (maker's mark); Lion passant (sterling standard); Crowned leopard head (London assay); Black letter capital K (date letter for 1765–66).

The bulbous body is raised on a round stepped base with a gadrooned edge and lip. The scroll handle is cast and applied.

65

Cream jug

BOSTON, MASSACHUSETTS, C. 1795
PRODUCED BY JOSEPH FOSTER (1760–1839)
H 5⅜ in. (13.7 cm), L 6⅜ in. (16.2 cm),
W 3¼ in. (8.3 cm)
71.803

Hallmarks (struck on bottom): FOSTER (maker's mark).

Raised on a stepped oval applied foot, this oval jug has an applied strap handle and a reeded band at the rim. The surface is plain except for the script initials EK engraved on the left side. Lit-

tle is known of Joseph Foster other than that he was apprenticed to Benjamin Burt, whose work is also in this volume. As Foster executed Burt's estate, they were probably good friends.

66

Cream jug

BOSTON, MASSACHUSETTS, C. 1795
PRODUCED BY JOSEPH LORING (1743–1815)
H 4½ in. (11.4 cm), L 5½ in. (14.0 cm),
W 2⅞ in. (7.3 cm)
71.810

Hallmarks (struck on bottom): J. LORING (maker's mark).

This oval helmet-shaped jug has an applied cast strap handle and is raised on an oval applied foot ring. A band is applied at the rim. A bright-cut cartouche of leafage appears on each side, and the left side bears the script initial B. Joseph Loring is thought to have been born in Hull, Massachusetts, and his work is close to that of Paul Revere II and Benjamin Burt, but there is no record of where he served his apprenticeship.

67

Cream jug

BOSTON, MASSACHUSETTS, C. 1795
PRODUCED BY SAMUEL WATERS
H 5½ in. (14.0 cm), L 5 in. (12.7 cm),
W 3⅛ in. (7.9 cm)
71.822

Hallmarks (struck on bottom): S.WATERS (maker's mark).

This elongated helmet-shaped jug with applied cast strap handle is raised on an oval applied foot and is decorated with bright cutting below the rim and a bright-cut shield engraved below the spout with the initial D. Samuel Waters was either apprenticed to or a good friend of Benjamin Burt, since Burt bequeathed his tools to Waters in 1805.

62

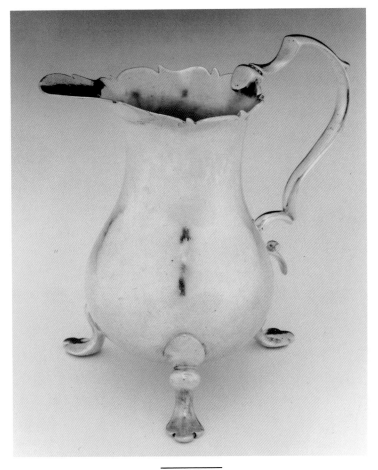

63

64

65

66

67

68

George III cream jug

LONDON, ENGLAND, 1808–9
PRODUCED BY JAMES MORISSET
H 3⅜ in. (8.6 cm), L 5¼ in. (13.3 cm),
W 3⅛ in. (7.9 cm)
78.70

Hallmarks (struck just under lip): I.M (maker's mark); Lion passant (sterling standard); Crowned leopard head (London assay); Roman capital N (date letter for 1808–9); King's head (duty stamp).

The body of this elliptical jug with a threaded lip and an applied cast handle is engraved with dotted and zigzag bands, as well as with a band of leaves suspended from a wavy dotted line. A cartouche of rows of dots forms an oval engraved with the conjoined initials AE in script. James Morisset was known for his fine work on gold boxes and presentation swords, in which he seems to have specialized. He was a Huguenot, and his French background is apparent in some of his extant works.

69

George III cream jug

LONDON, ENGLAND, 1803–4
PRODUCED BY JOHN EMES
H 3½ in. (8.9 cm), L 5½ in. (14.0 cm),
W 2¾ in. (7.0 cm)
ANONYMOUS GIFT IN MEMORY OF THE
HONORABLE JEFFERSON PATTERSON
78.7a

Hallmarks (struck in fluting at right side of handle): J.E (maker's mark); Lion passant (sterling standard); Crowned leopard head (London assay); Roman capital H (date letter for 1803–4); King's head (duty stamp).

The handle and lip of this oval helmet-shaped jug are both reeded. A cartouche and a Greek-key border are engraved just under the pouring lip, and there are bands of punchwork below this with heavy fluting around the bowl. The jug is raised on a slight oval foot rim, which, like the handle, is applied. The interior is gilded.

This cream jug is very much in the neoclassical style of the period, inspired by the archaeological excavations of Herculaneum and Pompeii in the mid-eighteenth century. The design of this particular jug was also inspired by the architectural and interior designs of Robert Adam, whose silver designs were a great influence on contemporary silversmiths, including John Emes. We know little of Emes except that his known work is very fine and that he paid one of the highest fees recorded for his apprenticeship to William Woollett in October of 1778—a sum of 105 pounds.

70

Covered sugar bowl

NORFOLK, VIRGINIA, C. 1835
PRODUCED BY JOSEPH M. FREEMAN (1806–82)
H 9 in. (22.9 cm), L 8½ in. (21.6 cm),
D 5¼ in. (13.3 cm)
GIFT IN HONOR OF MRS. HENRY CLAY
HOFHEIMER 85.22a–b

Hallmarks (struck on bottom): J. M. FREEMAN (maker's mark).

The body of this twelve-sided sugar bowl is raised on four applied feet comprised of C scrolls and shell motifs with leafage and openwork. It is plain except for the engraved coat of arms comprised of a shield surmounted by a mythological animal head and the motto Haud Muto Factum (Not Done by Muteness) on a ribbon. The cover has the same twelve-sided shape as the bowl, with a pumpkinlike finial applied.

The sugar bowl was probably made for Thomas G. Broughton of Norfolk, who was publisher of the Norfolk and Portsmouth Herald, a newspaper published from about 1794 until his death in 1861. The engraved coat of arms is that of the Delves-Broughton family of Doddington Park, Nantwich, Cheshire, to whom the Norfolk Broughtons traced themselves. These arms were created for Brian Broughton, who was knighted in March of 1660 and given the title Baronet of Broughton. One or more of the Broughton family immigrated to Virginia in the late seventeenth century, where they lived in what was then Princess Anne County.

71

Covered sugar bowl

BOSTON, MASSACHUSETTS, C. 1790
PRODUCED BY DAVID TYLER (1760–1804)
H 8½ in. (21.6 cm), L 6 in. (15.2 cm),
W 4½ in. (11.4 cm)
71.807a–b

Hallmarks (struck on side of foot): DT (maker's mark).

This paneled oval sugar bowl has an oval pedestal support resting on a shaped oval base. The lip is trimmed with fine beading, and the oval domed cover is surmounted with an urn-shaped finial.

68

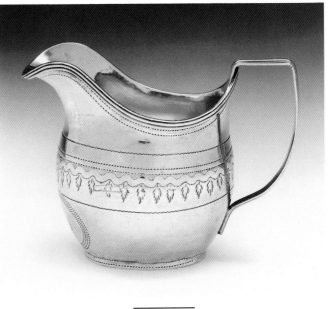

69

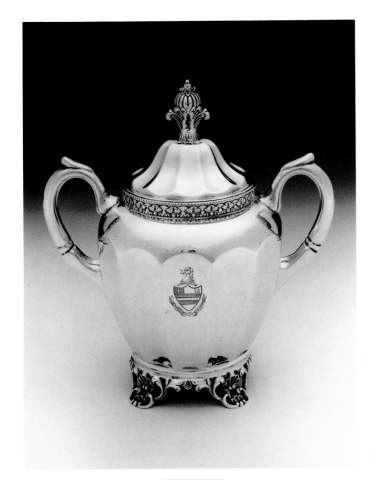

70

71

72

Cream jug

NORFOLK, VIRGINIA, C. 1791

PRODUCED BY JEREMIAH ANDREWS (D. 1817)

H 7½ in. (19.1 cm), L 5 in. (12.7 cm),
W 2⅝ in. (6.5 cm)

GIFT IN HONOR OF HENRY CLAY HOFHEIMER
FOR HIS YEARS OF WISE STEWARDSHIP OF THE
MUSEUM 83.596

Hallmarks (struck on front of base): NORFOLK, I. ANDREWS (place of production, maker's mark).

This helmet-shaped jug with an applied cast handle is raised on a square base with four ball feet. The round pedestal foot and the lip are decorated with gadrooning. Under the pouring spout is a cartouche with the conjoined script initials PCR. Hollowware made in Norfolk is extremely rare, and few known pieces exist today. This neoclassical-style cream jug and its companion sugar bowl (no. 73) show the influence of Philadelphia silversmiths on Andrews, who once worked in that city. Andrews went to New York from London, and later moved to Philadelphia, working there from 1776 until 1779. After living in Savannah, Georgia, for a time, he moved to Norfolk in 1791.

73

Covered sugar bowl

NORFOLK, VIRGINIA, C. 1791

PRODUCED BY JEREMIAH ANDREWS (D. 1817)

H 10 in. (25.4 cm), D 4¼ in. (10.8 cm)

GIFT IN HONOR OF HENRY CLAY HOFHEIMER
FOR HIS YEARS OF WISE STEWARDSHIP OF THE
MUSEUM 83.597a–b

Hallmarks (struck on base): NORFOLK, I. ANDREWS (place of production, maker's mark).

This covered urn-shaped bowl is raised on a round pedestal foot that rests on a square base. Gadrooning runs around the pedestal foot and the lip of the bowl, and two more bands appear on the cover, which is surmounted by a pineapple and a leaf finial. The bowl itself is surmounted by an applied gallery into which the loose cover fits. Engraved on the bowl is a cartouche with the conjoined initials PCR. This is a companion piece to no. 72.

74

Sugar bowl

NEWBURYPORT, MASSACHUSETTS, C. 1770

PRODUCED BY JOSEPH MOULTON (1724–95)

H 5⁷⁄₁₆ in. (13.8 cm), L 7⅞ in. (20.0 cm),
W 4⅜ in. (11.1 cm)

71.806

Hallmarks (struck on bottom): MOULTON (maker's mark).

This elliptical bowl with two cast and applied handles is decorated with bright-cut engraved bands of wavy lines, dotted lines, and swag and tassel around leaves. An engraved leafy cartouche has the script initials DD/to DH, while the cartouche on the reverse is blank. The bowl is raised on a plain oval applied foot rim, and the lip is finished with an applied threaded band.

75

Sugar bowl

BOSTON, MASSACHUSETTS, C. 1800

PRODUCED BY ROBERT EVANS (1768–1812)

H 3⅝ in. (9.2 cm), L 8¾ in. (22.2 cm),
W 4³⁄₁₆ in. (10.6 cm)

71.800

Hallmarks (struck on bottom): EVANS (maker's mark).

This elliptical bowl is raised on a threaded oval foot with a threaded lip, below which appears a serrated band and a band of Greek-key design. The conjoined initials AMT are engraved on the side. Two squared-off and threaded cast handles are applied.

76

George III tea urn

LONDON, ENGLAND, 1773–74

PRODUCED BY JAMES YOUNG

H 20 in. (50.8 cm), D 8⅛ in. (20.5 cm)

78.101

Hallmarks (struck on lip of cover and inside base where the removable body joins): I.Y (maker's mark); Lion passant (sterling standard); Crowned leopard head (London assay); Black letter capital S (date letter for 1773–74). Other marks (stamped on lip of cover): 103 . 6 (inventory number ?).

This tea urn with an ivory handle was designed in the neoclassical style for which James Young was known. It tapers down from a broad, round domed top to join the spool-shaped support, which is decorated with a band of leafage where it rests on the square base raised on four ball feet. The bottom of the body is decorated with a band of water leaves and chased with drapery swags terminating on each side in an applied cast satyr mask. Square hollow handles are applied to each side of the body. The cover and foot are engraved with a crest in the form of a dove, and there is an unidentified coat of arms engraved above the square spout. The cover terminates in an applied cast acorn.

A similar urn, now in a private collection in Philadelphia, was made by Richard Humphreys of Philadelphia in 1774, probably following the same design source as James Young. This urn is illustrated in *American Silver* by Graham Hood (1971, plate 174).

73   72

74

75

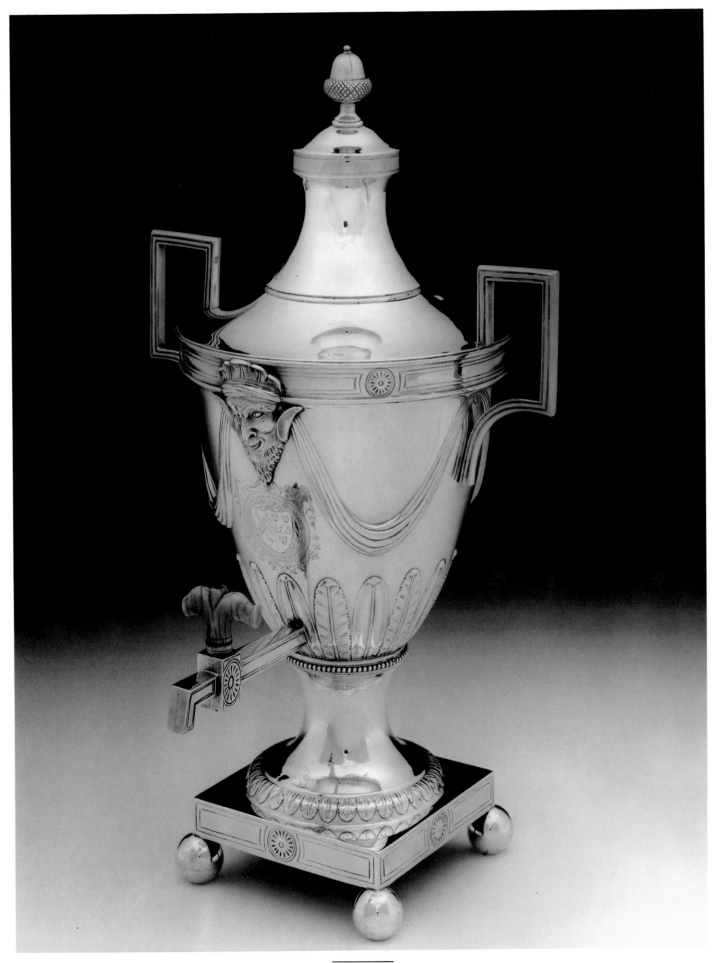

77

Kettle on stand

NEW YORK, NEW YORK, C. 1910
PRODUCED BY TIFFANY AND COMPANY
H 11½ in. (29.2 cm), L 6 in. (15.2 cm),
W 5¼ in. (13.3 cm)
GIFT OF THE BARONESS DE LUSTRAC 81.122a–c

Hallmarks (struck on bottom of kettle, burner, and stand): TIFFANY & CO./ MAKERS. (maker's mark); 1193 (pattern number); STERLING SILVER 925/1000 (silver standard); M (initial of John C. Moore, president of the company, 1907–47); 2 PINTS (measure on kettle only).

This octagonal kettle with applied spout has four applied lugs that allow it to fit onto its stand. There is a light openwork gallery around the top of the kettle. An applied hollow strap handle ends in stylized foliage with an ivory grip. The loose octagonal domed cover has an octagonal finial. The conjoined initials MCF are engraved on the back of the kettle, which has a raised octagonal base with a well for a spirit lamp. The stylized U-shaped supports of the kettle are attached to each side of the base.

78

George I tea caddy

LONDON, ENGLAND, 1718–19
PRODUCED BY JOHN FARNELL
H 5⅝ in. (11.8 cm), L 3⅛ in. (7.9 cm),
W 2 in. (5.1 cm)
78.83

Hallmarks: Badly rubbed, struck on cover slide: Lion's head erased (sterling standard); Heart-shaped mark (maker's mark). Struck on side of caddy: Roman capital C (date letter for 1718–19); Lion's head erased (sterling standard); Britannia (sterling standard). Struck on bottom: Heart with Fa (maker's mark); Engraved inscription: From/RICHARD NIXON/to/his God Daughter/ELIZABETH HAINES.

This is a plain rectangular tea caddy with canted corners. A slide top to fill the caddy is surmounted by a round domed cap to extract tea, with a ball finial on the cap. The stepped base is applied, as is the lip, and the slide has applied trim at one end.

79

Pair of George II tea caddies

LONDON, ENGLAND, 1756–57
PRODUCED BY SAMUEL TAYLOR
H 5¼ in. (13.3 cm), D 3¼ in. (8.3 cm)
78.114a–b

Hallmarks (struck on bottom of each): Crowned leopard head (London assay); Lion passant (sterling standard); Heart with ST (maker's mark); Black letter capital A (date letter for 1756–57).

These baluster-shaped caddies are chased with swirls, flowers, and leaves. Each caddy has an applied cast foot of flowers and C scrolls with openwork, and each top has a finial made of a cast flower applied to it. Unidentified coats of arms are engraved on the caddies. Samuel Taylor seems to have specialized in tea caddies and sugar bowls—his mark is seldom found on other objects. Decoratively chased flowers and leaves, of which he was perhaps overly fond, appear on much of his work.

77

78

79

Bibliography

Armelagos, George, and Peter Farb. *Consuming Passions: The Anthropology of Eating.* Boston: Houghton Mifflin Co., 1980.

Aron, Jean-Paul. *The Art of Eating in France: Manners and Menus in the Nineteenth Century.* Translated by Nina Rootes. London: Peter Owen Ltd., 1975.

Belden, Louise Conway. *Marks of American Silversmiths in the Ineson-Bissell Collection.* Charlottesville, Va.: University Press of Virginia for the Henry Francis du Pont Winterthur Museum, Winterthur, Del., 1980.

Beque, Émile. *Dictionnaire des Poinçons.* 3 vols. Paris: F. de Nobele, 1962.

Blair, Claude, ed. *The History of Silver.* New York: Ballantine Books, 1987.

de Bonneville, Françoise. *Jean Puiforcat.* Paris: Editions du Regard, 1986.

Brillat-Savarin, Jean Anthelme. *The Physiology of Taste, or Meditations on Transcendental Gastronomy.* Translated by M. F. K. Fisher. New York: Alfred A. Knopf, 1972.

Buhler, Kathryn C. *American Silver, 1655–1825, in the Museum of Fine Arts, Boston.* 2 vols. Greenwich, Conn.: New York Graphic Society for the Museum of Fine Arts, Boston, 1972.

Carpenter, Charles H., Jr. *Gorham Silver, 1831–1981.* New York: Dodd, Mead and Co., 1982.

Carpenter, Charles H., Jr., and Mary Grace Carpenter. *Tiffany Silver.* New York: Dodd, Mead and Co., 1978.

Clayton, Michael. *The Collector's Dictionary of the Silver and Gold of Great Britain and North America.* New York: World Publishing, 1971.

Cutten, George Barton. *The Silversmiths of Virginia, Together with Watchmakers and Jewelers, from 1694 to 1850.* Richmond, Va.: Dietz Press, 1952.

Davis, Frank. *French Silver, 1450–1825.* New York: Praeger Publishers, 1970.

Fales, Martha Gandy, *Early American Silver.* Rev. ed. New York: E.P. Dutton and Co., 1973.

Fales, Martha Gandy, and Henry N. Flynt. *The Heritage Foundation Collection of Silver, with Biographical Sketches of New England Silversmiths, 1625–1825.* Old Deerfield, Mass.: Heritage Foundation, 1968.

Fleming, John, and Hugh Honour. *Dictionary of the Decorative Arts.* New York: Harper and Row, 1977.

Garner, Philippe, ed. *The Encyclopedia of Decorative Arts, 1890–1940.* New York: Van Nostrand Reinhold, 1978.

Grimwade, Arthur G., F.S.A. *London Goldsmiths, 1697–1837, Their Marks and Lives from the Original Registers at Goldsmiths' Hall and Other Sources.* London: Faber and Faber, 1982.

Gruber, Alain. *L'Argenterie de maison du XVIe au XIXe siècle.* Fribourg: Office du Livre, 1982.

Haslam, Malcolm. *Marks and Monograms of the Modern Movement, 1875–1930.* New York: Charles Scribner's Sons, 1977.

Hood, Graham. *American Silver: A History of Style, 1650–1900.* New York: Praeger Publishers, 1971.

Hughes, Graham. *Modern Silver throughout the World, 1880–1967.* New York: Crown Publishers, 1967.

Jackson, Sir Charles James, F.S.A. *English Goldsmiths and Their Marks: A History of the Goldsmiths and Plate Workers of England, Scotland, and Ireland.* 2nd ed. New York: Dover Publications, 1964.

Kelley, Austin P. *The Anatomy of Antiques, A Collector's Guide.* New York: Viking Press, 1974.

Klein, Dan, and Margaret Bishop. *Decorative Art, 1880–1980.* Oxford: Phaidon-Christie's, 1986.

Klein, Dan, Nancy A. McClelland, and Malcolm Haslam. *In the Deco Style.* New York: Rizzoli International Publications, 1986.

Kovel, Ralph M., and Terry H. Kovel. *A Directory of American Silver, Pewter, and Silver Plate.* New York: Crown Publishers, 1979.

Lachmann, Ole. "Danish Silver Marks." *Silver,* March/April 1983, pp. 8–11.

McClinton, Katharine Morrison. *Art Deco, A Guide for Collectors.* New York: Clarkson N. Potter, 1972.

Mennell, Stephen. *All Manners of Food: Eating and Taste in England and France from the Middle Ages to the Present.* Oxford: Basil Blackwell Ltd., 1985.

Newman, Harold. *An Illustrated Dictionary of Silverware.* New York: Thames and Hudson, 1987.

Paulson, Paul L. *Guide to Russian Silver Hallmarks.* Washington, D.C.: Paul L. Paulson, 1976.

Rainwater, Dorothy T. *Encyclopedia of American Silver Manufacturers.* New York: Crown Publishers, 1975.

Revel, Jean-François. *Culture and Cuisine.* New York: Doubleday, 1982.

Smith, Georgiana Reynolds. *Table Decoration Yesterday, Today, and Tomorrow.* Rutland, Vt.: Charles E. Tuttle Co., 1968.

Tardy. *International Hallmarks on Silver Collected by Tardy.* Paris: Tardy, 1981.

Index